At the Heart of the Gospel

At the Heart of the Gospel

Suffering in the
Earliest Christian Message

L. Ann Jervis

William B. Eerdmans Publishing Company

Grand Rapids, Michigan / Cambridge, U.K.

Published 2007 by

Wm. B. Eerdmans Publishing Co.

2140 Oak Industrial Drive N.E., Grand Rapids, Michigan 49505 /

P.O. Box 163, Cambridge CB3 9PU U.K.

Printed in the United States of America

11 10 09 08 07   7 6 5 4 3 2 1

Library of Congress Cataloging-in-Publication Data

Jervis, L. Ann.

At the heart of the Gospel: suffering in the earliest Christian message / L. Ann Jervis.

p.   cm.

ISBN 978-0-8028-3993-0 (pbk. : alk. paper)

1. Suffering — Biblical teaching.

2. Bible. N.T. Thessalonians, 1st — Criticism, interpretation, etc.

3. Bible. N.T. Philippians — Criticism, interpretation, etc.

4. Bible. N.T. Romans — Criticism, interpretation, etc.

I. Title.

BS2725.6.S9J47   2007

233 — dc22

2006039044

www.eerdmans.com

In Memoriam
Shirley Eleanor Johnston
1930-2005

In Gratitude
Roy Dickson Hogg

Contents

Acknowledgments		xi
Prologue		xiii
1.	Introduction	1
	Suffering and the Approach of This Book	3
	Why This Investigation Matters	5
	The Organization and Scope of This Book	8
2.	1 THESSALONIANS	15
	Believer-Specific Suffering	15
	Paul's Reminder	15
	The Gospel Paul Proclaims Is Accompanied by Affliction	17
	The Shape of Affliction	18
	The Cause of Believer-Specific Suffering	22
	Suffering and Sanctification	24
	What Believer-Specific Suffering Is Not	26
	Suffering of Nonbelievers	27

CONTENTS

Summary   29

Using 1 Thessalonians to Talk about Suffering   30

Believer-Specific Suffering: The Challenge to Suffer   30

The Reasons for Believer-Specific Suffering   31

Our Suffering Is Productive   33

Joy   34

Suffering and Sanctification   35

The Suffering of Nonbelievers   35

Making Paul's Response to Nonbelievers Our Own   36

3. PHILIPPIANS   37

Suffering as a Believer   38

Philippians as an Apology for Suffering   42

Paul's Defense   45

Paul Exhorts the Philippians to Engage in the Same Struggle He Knows   61

The Communion of Suffering and Joy   62

Suffering of Nonbelievers   63

Summary   65

Using Philippians to Talk about Suffering   66

Assurance in Suffering   67

Philippians Offers Atypical Explanations for the Suffering of Believers   70

Is Christ to Blame?   73

Conclusion   74

4. ROMANS   77

Humanity's Shared Suffering   78

Sin Is a Power That Causes Suffering   79

Contents

Believers and Nonbelievers Have Distinct Relationships to Sin   82

Human Suffering in the Present   82

The Suffering of Lack of Trust in God's Righteousness   84

A History of Suffering   90

Suffering in the Future   90

Suffering as Humans "in Christ"   92

Suffering of Nonbelievers   92

Nonbelievers, Indentured to Sin, Help Spread Suffering   92

The Suffering of Those Who Do Not Believe in God   94

Nonbelievers, Whether Jew or Gentile, Create Suffering   96

Nonbelievers, Whether Jew or Gentile, Will Suffer   96

Nonbelievers, Whether Jew or Gentile, Will Be Subject to God's Wrath   97

The Suffering of Believers:
Suffering "in Christ" and "with Christ"   97

Another Context for Human Suffering: "in Christ"   98

"With Christ" Suffering   103

Suffering "with Christ" with Insight   108

Summary   114

Using Romans to Talk about Suffering   116

Suffering Is an Affront to Human Dignity   117

The Unity of Humanity   117

Paul's Concern for Those Not "in Christ"   118

Making Paul's Concern Our Own   119

Suffering "in Christ"   120

Suffering "with Christ": What It Means for Us, for God, and for God's Creation   122

CONTENTS

5. Conclusion   129

Speaking and Living the Heart of the Gospel:
Our Message   130

Our Response   132

    Suffering Is Wrong and to Be Resisted   132

    Resources "in Christ" to Respond to Suffering   133

    Our Hope   134

    Our Responsibility   134

Paul's Invitation   136

Index of Subjects and Names   139

Index of Scripture References   146

Acknowledgments

T his book took shape with the invaluable aid and nurturing challenges of members at the Center of Theological Inquiry, Prince-
ton, NJ. I thank fellow members of CTI during 2000-2001 and the fall of
2004 for helping me to articulate what I sensed was there to find in
Paul. I also thank Robert Jenson, Stephen Fowl, Robert Jewett, and Jo-
seph Mangina for their generosity in reading portions of my manu-
script with their inimitable insight and precision. My friend and col-
league Carol Finlay provided me with just the right questions as she
faithfully read through my work in progress. And my incomparable
husband Roy read through draft upon draft, giving me much wise
counsel springing from his deep well of Christian faith. My gratitude to
him is simply inexpressible. As always, my remarkable children Dylan
and Bronwen, with their capacities for love and life, occupy the front
row in my intended audience.

During the writing of this book my mother suffered greatly from
Parkinson's disease and finally died. This book is dedicated to her luminous example of how life, love, and joy can indeed shine through pain
and dying when one believes like Paul does.

Prologue

The genesis of this book is a collision in my life between my naïve understanding of the Christian faith as one that promises and expects happiness, and my experience of a degree of suffering in my adult years. Part of repairing from this collision has involved deep engagement with Paul, whom it is my privilege to study professionally as a biblical scholar. Not only did this book originate because my inherited Christian categories did not offer me enough room to explore and incorporate my experience of life's hardships, but a significant portion of the years spent actually writing this book has been spent in the vale of tears. The death of a marriage, the dying and death of my mother, the near death of my new husband, among other things, have made the subject of this book anything but an academic exercise for me. And, like most other people, the past few years have for me been deeply affected by the tragic events of our world. This book has taken shape in a world context severely scarred by suffering.

In what follows I unapologetically approach Paul's words as if they have the potential to mean something for the life I inhabit — my own and the lives of those within my horizon. I approach Paul's words as words of Scripture and as a fellow believer with Paul. I expect his words, desire his words, to speak some meaning into our experience of existence. It is hoped that, through careful attention to these words, this book will produce some light for our dark journey of suffering.

Moreover, given the absence in large quarters of western Christianity of rich reflection on suffering I consider it all the more important to hear (or to rehear) the foundational thoughts of Paul. His provocative and compelling insights into the predicament and importance of suffering call us to attention, and promise to help us actualize a kind of profound Christianity for which I believe our world longs.

1

INTRODUCTION

The presence of suffering is often understood as the absence of God; our response, whether intellectual or visceral, to suffering's cruel bite is to feel that God has abandoned us. This can be a particularly bitter and confusing experience for people of Christian faith. The disconnect between our faith in a caring and sovereign God and our experience of life's hardships almost inevitably poses a problem for us. For this reason among others, the following discussion is written in the first instance for believers in Christ and takes place in conversation with one of the earliest believers in Jesus Christ — Paul. I would, of course, be pleased if readers of other persuasions joined us.

This book's purpose is not to seek to justify suffering while also affirming the omnipotence and goodness of God. Neither is this book's interest in the origin of suffering — why a good God, who created the world, would allow suffering. Rather, the focus of this book is on learning from one of the chief architects of the Christian faith how we might respond to suffering.

Many great Christian minds have turned to the problems connected to the existence of suffering: its origin, its challenge to God's omnipotence and goodness and role as creator, and so on. Paul's focus was less on such issues and more on how now to live. In light of his uncompromising conviction that God in Christ has inaugurated the defeat of the cause of sufferings — sin, Paul's gaze is on the present in light of a future cleansed of travail.

Paul's energies are spent on moving the furniture of our minds and imaginations around so that we can see that our sufferings take place in a space embraced by God's love and that they are destined to be swallowed by glory. The task of this book is to describe in depth how, in three of his letters, Paul's faith in Jesus Christ shapes his reaction to the difficulties of human life (for both believers and nonbelievers) and then to think about how Paul's response might also be ours. I have chosen to be informed by Paul's reflections on suffering because of his obvious importance in the Christian constellation and because his position as one of the earliest believers in Christ to ponder this matter makes him immensely interesting to me.

THE FIRST PART of each of the following chapters is an analysis of what Paul says about suffering in particular letters. This includes conversation with other scholars on issues pertaining to the interpretation of the letters, and so this part of each chapter is fairly sprinkled with footnotes. It is, however, not essential to follow the discussion taking place at the level of the footnotes in order to make sense of my meaning.

In the second part of each chapter I reflect on how Paul's response to suffering might be understood or appropriated by us. Here I am enacting what I have come to see as an important and legitimate aspect of scholarly exegesis: to propose how, after careful and considered reading, a biblical text might take on meaning and life today.[1]

It also must be said that, though in each chapter's first part I am largely working in my normal territory — that of the professional biblical scholar — here too I have already stepped somewhat outside that territory. In the exegetical analysis I will guide our reading not with the traditional question "what did this text mean," but rather with the specific concern I have about how Paul, a believer in Jesus Christ, understood and responded to suffering. The type of exegetical work I do in

---

1. See L. A. Jervis, "Freeing Exegesis," in *Character Ethics and the New Testament,* ed. R. L. Brawley (Louisville: Westminster John Knox, 2007), pp. 87-106.

the first part of each chapter, then, begins not with the text but with me the interpreter, with my concern.

K. Stendahl's well-known stage one of the interpretative process — asking what the text meant — a stage that must, in his view, be separate from stage two, asking what the text means[2] — is not the model for my chapters. I begin where I am, not where the text is. I understand that the distance between the past of the text and my present as an interpreter is already bridged on the pylons of my concern and my expectation that Paul's words can be useful for the life of faith. While I will proceed in the first part of each chapter with the tools of critical biblical scholarship and so seek to discipline my interpretation such that I allow myself to hear the surprising or unwanted, nevertheless to a degree I recognize that the past and present are fused in the energy of my interest about a matter that touches our present lives. At the same time, this fusion does not obliterate the entities involved — me as the interpreter with my interests and the text of Paul. These two entities remain separate while not being locked in their foreign worlds. And, because they exist in the same circle of meaning, these two entities may radiate off each other.[3]

Both parts of each chapter — exegesis and proposing how to use what I have seen — are shaped by my concern to find ways to respond with hope, peace, and action in the face of suffering.

Suffering and the Approach of This Book

Before proceeding, it is important to indicate the meaning of the word "suffering" in this inquiry. While some would distinguish between pain

2. K. Stendahl, "Biblical Theology, Contemporary," in *The Interpreter's Dictionary of the Bible* (New York: Abingdon, 1962), I, pp. 418-32.

3. My assumption is that while the biblical authors and the contemporary interpreter live in different times and cultures, which necessarily affects their faith, there is enough of a kinship of faith that the exegete and the biblical author may be said to stand in the same "aura of meaning." Cf. Ricoeur: "No interpreter . . . come(s) close to what his text says if he does not live in the aura of meaning that is sought" (*The Conflict of Interpretations: Essays in Hermeneutics* [Evanston: Northwestern University Press, 1974], p. 298).

and suffering, the first referring to discomfort of the body and the second to disease in the mind and spirit,[4] I will follow the definition of suffering as that which is endured[5] in either body, mind, or spirit as a result of that which is distressing, injurious, or painful.[6] Such suffering includes pain, death, punishment, hardship, disaster, grief, sorrow, care, loneliness, injury, loss, shame, disgrace, bodily injury or discomfort, disease, etc.[7]

I recognize the risk of minimizing the differences between the type of suffering of which I am aware and the type Paul experienced and pondered, both in his own life and in the lives of those to whom he writes. The obvious danger is that, in my eagerness to bring Paul's words into conversation with my concern and vice versa, I will diminish particularities. Perhaps the only response to this danger is to be aware of it.

It must be added that this book is undertaken more with a hermeneutics of sympathy than a hermeneutics of suspicion.[8] Consequently, in the course of interpreting Paul my interest will be in hearing what he believes rather than in judging whether his beliefs are right or spending much time analyzing what agenda might be behind his words.

It must also be said that this book works on the presupposition that Paul has something relevant to say to fellow believers. And I share with other premodern Christian thinkers and with some contemporary bib-

---

4. So J. A. Amato, *Victims and Values: A History and a Theory of Suffering* (Contributions in Philosophy 42; New York: Greenwood, 1999), p. 14.

5. The Latin roots of the word imply being weighed down under; suffering is something we bear or endure.

6. So, *Oxford English Dictionary*, "Suffer." For a similar willingness to include bodily pain in the category of suffering, see the interesting work of the physician Adrian C. Moulyn, *The Meaning of Suffering: An Interpretation of Human Existence From the Viewpoint of Time* (Contributions in Philosophy 22; Westport: Greenwood, 1982).

7. Again, *OED,* "Suffer."

8. A hermeneutics of sympathy (my terminology) has sympathy with the author and reads along with the author's thoughts and believes, in the sense of being a sympathetic listener, what the author says. A hermeneutics of suspicion, which is more typical of biblical scholarship, strives for a critical distance from the text so that issues of the author's bias, rhetorical ploys, and historical reasons for a certain presentation of matters may be explored.

lical scholars[9] the expectation that Paul's words, as Scripture, can be heard well with ears of faith.[10]

This book will investigate three of Paul's letters on a particular theme: the theme of suffering. It is important to note this thematic approach at the outset in order to position my exegetical work in relation to the commentary tradition. My focus on the theme of suffering necessarily means that, as I highlight this aspect of Paul's thought, I will not take notice of many other things he says. It is however hoped, and I do intend, that what I say about the theme of suffering in each letter fits intelligently with that letter's other features.

Why This Investigation Matters

Preventative Reasons

The texts on suffering in the New Testament have the potential to harm and distort human health — physical, spiritual, and mental. In this regard, let me give an anecdote from my experience as an Anglican priest. The lectionary reading for a service at which I preached was Matt 10:34-39:

> Do not think that I have come to bring peace on earth; I have not come to bring peace, but a sword. For I have come to set a man against his father, and a daughter against her mother, and a daughter-in-law against her mother-in-law; and a man's foes will

9. E.g., S. Fowl, *Engaging Scripture: A Model for Theological Interpretation* (Malden: Blackwell, 1998); F. Watson, *Text and Truth* (Grand Rapids: Eerdmans, 1997); idem, *Text, Church and World: Biblical Interpretation in Theological Perspective* (Grand Rapids: Eerdmans, 1994).

10. I am not arguing that the Bible can or should be read only by people of faith, or that only people of faith can understand the Bible. I do, however, resist the view that people of faith are necessarily imprisoned by what A. Schweitzer, referring to the church's traditional interpretation of the life of Jesus, termed the "stony rocks of ecclesiastical doctrine" (*The Quest of the Historical Jesus* [Baltimore: Johns Hopkins University Press, 1998], p. 399), unable to connect intelligently with the biblical text.

be those of his own household. He who loves father or mother more than me is not worthy of me; and he who loves son or daughter more than me is not worthy of me; and he who does not take his cross and follow me is not worthy of me. He who finds his life will lose it, and he who loses his life for my sake will find it. (NRSV)

The first person to approach me after the service was a woman who comes to the food bank at our church. Agnes suffers from mental illness that in her case involves self-loathing and self-destructive behavior. Without a word of greeting, Agnes looked cheerfully into my eyes and asked, "Do you know where I can get a hair shirt?"[11]

Her question reminded me of how careful the teacher, exegete, preacher, pastoral leader, fellow Christian must be with the NT passages about suffering. It is my opinion that these passages have been, are, and can be heard and used in ways that are contrary to the good news of which they are a part. Communication is always delicate and imperfect, and we cannot control how our words will be heard or used. However, considered thought about NT passages on suffering seems a wise venture given that these texts may touch the most sensitive of human wounds and fears. These passages are unruly. Their power to leap out from the context of the good news and stand on their own as justification of suffering or command to suffer, often without reference to the whole of the gospel, means that they require extra interpretive attention.

In the following investigation we will find that Paul accepted that believers would suffer. This fact makes patient, even painstaking study of his words all the more essential. For, unless such ideas are heard as well as we possibly can, a shallow understanding of them may justify precisely the kind of suffering that it is our role as Christians to alleviate. And, unless these texts are heard well, our misreading may encourage us to avoid precisely the kind of suffering he is calling us to embrace. A litany of Christian martyrs and apologists who have appealed to Paul's words for arguably misguided actions and advice could be

---

11. A hair shirt is a shirt made of haircloth worn against the skin by ascetics and penitents for the purpose of self-mortification.

given, but it is a better use of energy to proceed on the basis that Paul's thoughts are important for fellow believers and, consequently, so is attentive reading of his words.

Moreover, when understood shallowly, or misunderstood, these texts are unable to speak *for* the gospel. The consequence of this is that conversation with people who do not share our faith about matters as significant as violence and the sacred, or death, may not benefit from what Christianity offers.[12] Careful attention to what Paul says may serve to avoid misguided communication between Christians and people of other orientations on the matter of suffering.

Productive Reasons

Not only is it valuable to study Paul's understanding of suffering for preventative reasons, but also for what may be called productive reasons. Our experience of suffering almost always leads us to ask, among other things, "why" and "how long." And for some Christian believers, the Bible is a place to look for answers. Another reason for the labor of this investigation is a conviction that an awareness of what at least portions of the NT say about suffering may helpfully illuminate our own experience of suffering.

An Investigation Waiting to Happen

The third reason for what follows is that, in my view, it is an investigation begging to be done. While each of the passages to be investigated

12. For instance, R. Girard's provocative theory about the role of violence in human society and about primitive religion's identification of violence and the sacred will be better tested on the Christian texts (Girard claims he hopes his theory will be tested on the Judeo-Christian texts; *Violence and the Sacred,* tr. P. Gregory [Baltimore: Johns Hopkins University Press, 1972], p. 309) if these texts have been carefully elucidated on the matter at hand. (This is not to imply a critique of those, like R. Hamerton-Kelly, who have engaged Girard's theory with Paul.)

has received, like the rest of the NT, numerous conscientious exegeses, as far as I am aware, neither the organizational task which I will undertake (and shortly describe) nor the attempt to combine exegesis of particular biblical books with talk in the present tense about suffering has been carried out.

The Organization and Scope of This Book

This book will organize Pauline passages about suffering into two categories: texts that speak of the suffering experienced by human beings who reject Christ or do not know him, and those that address the suffering that accrues only to believers in Jesus Christ. I undertake this organizational task because my reading of Paul (and of other parts of the NT) has led me to understand that the early believers who authored the NT viewed matters in this way. We will see in our study of Paul that he thinks there is suffering specific to those who do not believe in Jesus.[13] And we will see him pondering the fact that believers in Jesus continue to experience the troubles of human existence and reckoning with the idea that believers take on a suffering particular to them that is positively connected to God's redeeming humanity and all creation from suffering. In order to reflect what I believe to be Paul's own distinctions I have chosen to organize my inquiry by identifying which passages from his letters speak about believers' suffering and which about the sufferings of nonbelievers.

If we had space, we might see a comparable view in the early parts of Matthew and Luke.[14] There we find that the suffering of those who welcome Jesus is alleviated at the cost of Jesus' disciples, who take on

13. For instance, Paul promises nonbelievers God's wrath in the "day of the Lord."

14. Much New Testament scholarship accepts the hypothesis that Matthew and Luke used two main sources in compiling their Gospels: Mark and Q. Many of the passages on suffering found now in Matthew and Luke belong to the source Q. For example, the passage cited above from Matt 10:34-39 is part of the hypothetical Q document. See J. M. Robinson, P. Hoffmann, and J. S. Kloppenborg, *The Critical Edition of Q* (Hermeneia; Minneapolis: Fortress, 2000).

additional hardships. Disciples of Jesus, those who are invited to take up their cross and follow him, are pledged suffering in the course of their task of extending God's healing reign.[15] It is at the cost of disciples' suffering that those who are open to Jesus and his disciples have their sufferings taken away. Had we time to investigate these texts we would also see that they speak of suffering particular to those who reject Jesus and the reign of God.

As should by now be clear, the task of this book goes beyond categorization to interpretation. After determining which texts belong to which category, the task of seeking to understand what they might mean will be undertaken. I use the word "might" willfully. I am committed in this investigation to the task of the scholar of the Bible, a task I take to be focused on coming to a reasonable proposition about what the author of a particular passage *might* be seeking to communicate. I am thus acknowledging that I value what the author (Paul) wanted to say, that I believe it is possible to know something of what that was, and that I recognize that the understanding to which I come is in the final analysis only a proposal.[16]

There is also another reason that I use the word "might." I do so because, as stated, I am committed in this book to overstepping the traditional bounds of the biblical scholar. I will ask how the texts I study *might* be used in our conversations and interactions with other Christian believers on the matter of suffering. It is at this point that my stepping beyond the bounds takes me into vulnerable territory. For at the point at which I work outside the parameters of biblical scholarship I have no professionally legitimate way to validate my insights; they are not the observations of a trained systematician or philosopher or ethicist or social scientist. They are *amateur* reflections.

I choose the word "amateur" for both its colloquial pejorative sense

---

15. See L. A. Jervis, "Suffering in the Reign of God: The Persecution of Disciples in Q," *Novum Testamentum* 44 (2001): 3-20; also idem, "All for Jesus: The Cause, Character and Role of Discipleship Suffering in Q," *Pro Ekklesia* 11 (2002): 41-56.

16. Such provisionality here is affirmed by postmodernism's insight that interpretative objectivity is impossible, that the quest for one true meaning is fruitless and illusory, and that the interpreter can never escape her own horizons.

and its root meaning. I admit, borrowing the words of C. S. Lewis, that "if any real theologian reads these pages he will very easily see that they are the work of a layman and an amateur."[17] At the same time, I affirm that I am an amateur in the best sense of that word. My reflections in the latter part of each chapter are those of "one who loves." Although inadequately, I love God through Jesus Christ, I love pondering the divine and our humanity in company with the words of Scripture, and I love my and our humanity. It is the combination of these loves that makes for me the matter of suffering so riveting.

In the last generation the distinguished philosopher and theologian Arthur C. McGill produced a significant and honest book on suffering in which he stated some views on the work of theology and the role of the interpreter of Scripture that resonate with my enterprise.[18] I found his book after producing what follows and before trying to describe what it was I had done in the second part of each chapter. McGill states that "theology, as an activity of the understanding, represents a responsible effort to celebrate and share in the light of God, to gather the broken and clouded fragments of human existence into the radiant openness that Christ brings. That is why theology is not an activity restricted to the experts. It is to be undertaken by everyone who knows Christ as the light of the world and who exercises his understanding to participate in that light and to share it with others."[19]

My efforts to propose ways that particular biblical texts may be connected to the present experience of suffering may be understood as attempts at what McGill calls "problematic theology." McGill distinguishes between biblical theology, which focuses on sorting out the obscurities of the scriptural text; dogmatic theology, which describes the content of Christian revelation and what various Christian thinkers have proposed about its meaning; and "problematic theology," which "consciously seeks the light of Christ in terms of a specific problem of human existence."[20]

17. *The Problem of Pain* (London: Centenary, 1940), p. viii.
18. A. C. McGill, *Suffering: A Test of Theological Method* (Philadelphia: Geneva, 1968; reprint Philadelphia: Westminster, 1982).
19. *Suffering*, p. 26.
20. *Suffering*, p. 123.

If the work of the latter part of each chapter needs a category, this one may well suit. I seek to make suggestive connections between the problem of suffering which we all know in one way or another, and the Pauline letter just studied. I offer these suggestions not in the belief that I have always made the right connections or that what I say is conclusive, but rather in confidence that it is important to try to hear the words of Scripture speaking in a manner that is both respectful of the fact that they were not written with us in mind and alive to the possibility that the kinship of faith we share with the authors of the Bible may illuminate the fragments of our own lives.

There are numerous passages on suffering in the NT, indeed in the Bible as a whole. Studies of the theme of suffering in the Bible recognize the fact that the Bible has different responses to the fact of suffering.[21] What I offer in this study is an opportunity to ponder three letters of Paul in what I consider is a novel way.

The Pauline letters I will read are 1 Thessalonians, Philippians, and Romans. In a perfect world this book would investigate the entire Pauline corpus and indeed the whole NT. In fact, once a person begins to think about suffering when she is reading the Bible, the passages to be investigated and contemplated in both the Old and New Testaments are almost endless. However, practicalities demand that there be limits, and the limits I have chosen for this book are to read only three letters of Paul. One might ask, if one is to read Paul, why not include the Corinthian correspondence, which is rife with references to suffering. My answer is that, as there is already a substantial and valuable literature on the topic of suffering in 1 and 2 Corinthians, I consider it a better use of time and energy to focus on other letters.[22]

---

21. See, for instance, J. C. Beker, *Suffering and Hope: The Biblical Vision and the Human Predicament* (Grand Rapids: Eerdmans, 1987); and earlier E. F. Sutcliffe, *Providence and Suffering in the Old and New Testaments* (London: Nelson, 1953).

22. See, for instance, J. T. Fitzgerald, *Cracks in an Earthen Vessel: An Examination of the Catalogues of Hardships in the Corinthian Correspondence* (Atlanta: Scholars, 1988); K. A. Plank, *Paul and the Irony of Affliction: A Literary and Rhetorical Analysis of 1 Corinthians 4:9-13* (Atlanta: Scholars, 1987); A. E. Harvey, *Renewal through Suffering: A Study of 2 Corinthians* (Edinburgh: Clark, 1996); S. J. Hafemann, *Suffering and Ministry in the*

The three letters chosen each offer a particular perspective on believers' suffering which together suggest a rich response to it. Put all too briefly: in 1 Thessalonians Paul challenges believers to recognize that acceptance of the gospel is acceptance of suffering; in Philippians Paul contemplates, defends, and describes suffering as a believer; and in Romans, Paul emphasizes that believers share the human lot, while illuminating the unique context in which we do so "in Christ" and clarifying our obligation to take on additional sufferings "with Christ" for the sake of God's creation. This can be understood as a three-step progression:[23] in 1 Thessalonians Paul challenges believers to recognize suffering as part of the vocation of the Christian, in Philippians he offers a rich conceptual context for understanding this vocation, and in Romans he offers an understanding of how we may both undergo the challenges that come to every human and participate in reducing suffering's bite.

While Paul's views on the suffering of nonbelievers are less fulsome and nuanced than are his views on believers' suffering, they are nevertheless concerned and compassionate. In 1 Thessalonians, nonbelievers are not much in Paul's sightlines, although he implicitly expresses concern about the difficulty of undergoing present human suffering without faith. In Philippians Paul's focus on suffering as a believer almost obliterates from his view the plight of nonbelievers. When Paul does briefly turn an eye to nonbelievers, it is to their future suffering if they remain "enemies of the cross of Christ." As I read him,

---

Spirit: Paul's Defense of His Ministry in 2 Corinthians 2:14–3:3 (Grand Rapids: Eerdmans, 1990); T. B. Savage, *Power through Weakness: Paul's Understanding of the Christian Ministry in 2 Corinthians* (Cambridge: Cambridge University Press, 1996).

23. Whether or not this progress is chronological — as in the sequential development of Paul's thinking — is not critical to this inquiry. (The matter of the chronological sequence of Paul's letters is still unsettled in Pauline scholarship. See the helpful appendix on this topic in C. J. Roetzel, *Paul: The Man and the Myth* [Columbia: University of South Carolina Press, 1998], pp. 178-83.) While I happen to hold the majority view that Romans was written after Philippians and 1 Thessalonians before Philippians, that is not the reason for the order of this book. It is rather for the heuristic value of organizing Paul's thoughts on suffering into something of a pattern that the book is ordered as it is.

Paul hopes that all such enmity will be resolved. In Romans, on the other hand, Paul expresses a concern so profound and broad for the tribulations of humanity that it would be criminal to summarize it here.

Paul's thoughts on the predicament and the importance of suffering have provided raw material from which the greatest of Christian thinkers (Irenaeus, Augustine, Aquinas, Luther, Calvin, Barth, and so on) fashioned influential and substantial frameworks for reckoning with life in our suffering-infused environment. On the other hand, as the prevalence of health and wealth gospels indicates, much contemporary Christianity has chosen to ignore or reposition Paul's thoughts on suffering. In what follows I will seek to hear Paul's words in their undeveloped and primary freshness in hopes of allowing my readers to be deeply marked, like the saints and shapers of our faith, by the power of Paul's gospel — a gospel of which we need not be ashamed precisely because it is not easy.

2

1 THESSALONIANS
An Uncomfortable Joy

Believer-Specific Suffering

Paul's Reminder

In this letter to a group of people whom Paul says "turned to God from idols" (1:9)[1] the topic of suffering surfaces almost immediately. In the course of giving thanks (1:2-10)[2] Paul states that the Thessalonians became imitators both of himself, Silvanus, and Timothy and of the Lord. The circumstances of this imitation were, Paul says, their receiving of the word in much θλίψις (affliction), with joy from the Holy Spirit (1:6).

Paul here signals that he understands suffering to be part of the

1. For a proposal about the type of religious and civic cultic practices and beliefs the Thessalonians may have been nurtured in, see K. P. Donfried, "The Cults of Thessalonica and the Thessalonian Correspondence," *New Testament Studies* 31 (1985): 336-56 = *Paul, Thessalonica, and Early Christianity* (Grand Rapids: Eerdmans, 2002), pp. 21-49.

2. Though many include only 1:2-5 in the first thanksgiving period (e.g., P. T. O'Brien, *Introductory Thanksgivings in the Letters of Paul* [Novum Testamentum Supplements 49; Leiden: Brill, 1977], pp. 146-53), I understand the first thanksgiving section to be 1:2-10 (see L. A. Jervis, *The Purpose of Romans: A Comparative Letter Structure Investigation* [Journal for the Study of the New Testament Supplement Series 55; Sheffield: Sheffield Academic, 1991], pp. 91-94).

warp and woof of the gospel, that acceptance of the gospel is at the same time acceptance of suffering. Suffering is not an accidental by-product of believing in Jesus Christ. Rather, suffering is intrinsic to the good news, for, in Calvin's rendition, believers are "appointed to it."[3] Paul is concerned here that his readers understand that their current experience of persecution is not unexpected.

Paul emphasizes that when he preached the gospel, he preached also the requirement of suffering.[4] Here Paul's words on suffering are both reactive and reiterative. He is reacting to the Thessalonians' trying situation by reminding them of what he has told them. Paul calls his converts' attention to the type of gospel they received — when they accepted the gospel they accepted also suffering. While clearly Paul is responding to a new situation (3:6), he is at pains to clarify for his converts that this new situation is really only another manifestation of what they have already experienced and what they already know: he told them from the start that by receiving the good news they would experience also affliction (3:4), and they in fact encountered this at their conversion (1:6). Paul seeks to encourage the Thessalonians in their troubles by reminding them that this is the package they accepted: the gospel is wrapped not just in joy, but also in affliction.

Both the first time Paul expresses his thankfulness (1:2-10) and the second (2:13-16),[5] Paul describes what the Thessalonians have known

---

3. *Commentaries on the Epistles to the Philippians, Colossians and Thessalonians*, tr. J. Pringle (Grand Rapids: Eerdmans, 1948), p. 266.

4. See L. A. Jervis, "Accepting Affliction: Paul's Preaching on Suffering" in *Character and Scripture: Moral Formation, Community, and Biblical Interpretation*, ed. W. P. Brown (Grand Rapids: Eerdmans, 2002), pp. 290-316.

5. I regard 2:13-16 also as a thanksgiving (cf. J. C. Hurd, "Concerning the Structure of 1 Thessalonians," in *The Earlier Letters of Paul and Other Studies* [Frankfurt: Lang, 1998], p. 82) and accept the authenticity of 2:14-16. On this last point, see particularly the arguments against B. A. Pearson, "1 Thessalonians 2:13-16: A Deutero-Pauline Interpolation," *Harvard Theological Review* 64 (1971): 79-84, in C. J. Schlueter, *Filling Up the Measure: Polemical Hyberbole in 1 Thessalonians 2:14-16* (Journal for the Study of the New Testament Supplement Series 98; Sheffield: JSOT, 1994); and in K. P. Donfried, "Paul and Judaism: 1 Thessalonians 2:13-16 as a Test Case," *Interpretation* 38 (1984): 242-53. For review of scholarship that argues for the letter's unity, see R. Riesner, *Paul's Early Pe-*

from the moment they accepted the gospel: they have known suffering (2:14). Their current suffering should, then, not be surprising (3:3-4). Not only, as we have noted, did the Thessalonians know affliction when they received the gospel, but the people from whom they received the gospel were themselves sufferers (2:2).[6]

The Gospel Paul Proclaims Is Accompanied by Affliction

In 1:6 Paul states that the Thessalonians "became imitators of us and of the Lord, for you received the word (ὁ λόγος) in much affliction, with joy inspired by the Holy Spirit." The commentary tradition correctly assumes that ὁ λόγος refers to the proclamation of the gospel.[7] This is a reasonable assumption, since in the previous verse Paul speaks of "the word" as an aspect of the gospel. There Paul states that the gospel's presence is rightly manifest when its word is surrounded by power, the Holy Spirit, and full certainty (1:5). Such a manifestation of the gospel's presence occurs when it is rightly received — received in the way the Lord, and the Lord's servants, received it: in much affliction with the Holy Spirit's joy. That Paul should speak of the Lord receiving the word is strongly suggestive of the human Jesus' acceptance of God's mission for him. Elsewhere Paul refers to the faith of Jesus (e.g., Rom 3:22; Gal 2:16; 3:22; Phil 3:9).[8] Here Paul may be alluding to Jesus' faith, holding

---

riod: *Chronology, Mission Strategy, Theology,* tr. D. Stott (Grand Rapids: Eerdmans, 1998), pp. 409-11.

6. I accept V. C. Pfitzner's understanding that Paul's reference to πολλῷ ἀγῶνι in 2:2 is to "the opposition which accompanied the preaching of Paul and his companions" (*Paul and the Agon Motif: Traditional Athletic Imagery in the Pauline Literature* [Leiden: Brill, 1967], p. 113).

7. See, e.g., Calvin, *The Epistles of Paul to the Romans and Thessalonians,* tr. R. Mackenzie (Calvin's New Testament Commentaries; Grand Rapids: Eerdmans, 1973), p. 337; F. F. Bruce, *1 and 2 Thessalonians* (Word Biblical Commentary; Waco: Word, 1982), p. 14; E. Best, *A Commentary on the First and Second Epistles to the Thessalonians* (New York: Harper and Row Publishers, 1972), p. 77.

8. The phrase πίστις Χριστοῦ can be read as either an objective genitive — faith *in* Christ, or a subjective genitive — faith *of* Christ. In recent years many scholars, myself

up Jesus' way of accepting the word — his faith — as paradigmatic. What Paul draws attention to is the obvious fact that Jesus' acceptance of the word was accompanied by affliction, albeit this affliction was also accompanied by the peculiar joy that only the Holy Spirit can inspire.

Paul responds to the Thessalonians' current suffering by reminding them that they received the gospel like the Lord did, thereby affirming their imitation of Christ.[9] Paul's gratitude to God for the manner in which the Thessalonians received the good news is at the same time a reminder to his converts of the complexity of being loved by God. Being God's beloved (1:4) does not mean protection from affliction, yet it does mean joy. Jesus is the chief example of this reality.

The Shape of Affliction

The particular form that suffering took for the Thessalonian believers appears to have involved rejection by compatriots (2:14-16).[10] However, as Paul makes clear in his first thanksgiving, the *fundamental* shape of the affliction involved in the gospel is the shape of Christ's afflictions.

Paul does not flesh out the nature of Christ's afflictions as they relate to believers' afflictions, but indications in this letter are that Paul understood the sufferings of Christ to be related positively to the birthing of the new age. For one thing, Paul chooses the word θλίψις to describe

---

included, have opted for the latter. See especially R. B. Hays, *The Faith of Jesus Christ: An Investigation of the Narrative Substructure of Galatians 3:1–4:11* (Society of Biblical Literature Dissertation Series 56; Chico: Scholars, 1983); M. D. Hooker, "ΠΙΣΤΙΣ ΧΡΙΣΤΟΥ" *New Testament Studies* 35 (1989): 321-42; D. A. Campbell, *The Rhetoric of Righteousness in Romans 3:21-26* (Journal for the Study of the New Testament Supplement Series 65; Sheffield: JSOT, 1992); and I. Wallis, *The Faith of Jesus Christ in Early Christian Tradition* (Cambridge: Cambridge University Press, 1995).

9. Cf. J. S. Pobee, *Persecution and Martyrdom in the Theology of Paul* (Journal for the Study of the New Testament Supplement Series 6; Sheffield: JSOT, 1985), p. 109. W. P. de Boer makes the important observation that the character of imitation is "a bringing to expression in their own lives of what they had seen and detected outside themselves" (*The Imitation of Paul: An Exegetical Study* [Kampen: Kok, 1962], p. 124).

10. See above for argument in favor of the authenticity of this passage.

both Christ's and believers' suffering (1:6; cf. his use of πάθημα elsewhere, e.g., Phil 3:10). This word was used for a woman's birth pangs (e.g., John 16:21). Passages in Jewish writings (e.g., *1 Enoch* 62:4; *4 Ezra* 4:42) and in Paul (e.g., 1 Thess 5:3; Rom 8:22) use the image of birthing to describe the emergence of the day of the Lord. Given the eschatological ring of Paul's initial proclamation to the Thessalonians as he records it in this letter (1:9-10), Paul may have understood Christ's afflictions as the pangs required to bring forth God's new age. Those who imitate Christ share in these birth pangs. Therefore, while the good news promises eternal life (4:14-17; 5:10) and escape from the wrath to come (1:10; 5:9), it also requires that now believers wait (1:10). And, in the waiting is suffering, for we are waiting for the full emergence of the new age. We are in the throes of θλίψις, of giving birth. Just as Jesus' suffering contributed to the birth of the new age, so does the suffering of believers.

Intimations from 1 Thessalonians, then, are that believers' suffering is an aspect of our participation in God's work of bringing forth the new age. Believers share in the birthing process initiated by Jesus, and so know afflictions.

Adding up the indications in the letter — that Paul's initial gospel was eschatologically focused, that he uses the word θλίψις, which apocalyptic literature uses in its imagery for the emergence of the day of the Lord, and that he uses the image of the pains of childbirth to speak of the period of waiting for God's deliverance — we might say that Paul understood the suffering of believers to be necessary to bringing God's salvific project to completion. But this might seem to make too much out of too little. There is, however, another indicator that may strengthen or confirm this reading.

Paul commends his converts for exhibiting faith, love, and hope during this time of waiting for salvation. He directly links the perseverance of hope to Christ (1:3)[11] and throughout the letter presents hope

---

11. As J. E. Frame notes, "the genitives are somewhat bewildering and the interpretations are various" (p. 76). He, like most commentators, decides that τοῦ κυρίου ἡμῶν Ἰησοῦ Χριστοῦ is an objective genitive qualifying ἐλπίδος (*A Critical and Exegetical Commentary on the Epistles of St. Paul to the Thessalonians* [Edinburgh: Clark, 1912]).

along with faith and love as a "triad of graces."[12] Consequently, the efforts undertaken for faith and love are linked to Christ just as is the perseverance of hope. For Paul the faith, love, and hope the Thessalonians exercise are rooted in Christ. These are, then, Christ-like characteristics, what Calvin calls "God's manifestation of Himself . . . through the gifts of His Spirit."[13]

Paul commends the Thessalonians for presently exhibiting these Christ-like dispositions (1:3), but he also encourages his converts to increase them.[14] He sees this increase as essential to his converts' sanctification, and he sees their sanctification as critical in relation to the "coming of the Lord Jesus" (3:12-13). He repeatedly expresses to the Thessalonians his urgent desire that their faith, hope, and love blossom into holiness in time for the coming of the Lord Jesus. Their holiness — their faith, hope, and love[15] — has a future focus: it will allow them to gain salvation (5:8-9).

Faith, hope, and love also have an effect in this time of waiting for deliverance from the coming wrath (1:10). Now faith, hope, and love garner to themselves suffering. For Paul, sanctification and suffering are of a piece during this time of waiting. It is, Paul says, a temptation to think otherwise, a temptation so serious that to give into it would be to lose the hope of salvation (3:5).

Paul understands the threads of holiness, which are faith, hope, and love, to be threaded through the needle of affliction. Living in faith, hope, and love does not mean that one is protected from pains. In fact, quite the opposite. By accepting the word of the gospel (1:6) and determining to lead lives worthy of God (2:12), the Thessalonians became both people who exhibited faith, hope, and love and people who suffered. Their faith, hope, and love are expressed as they suffer. Receiving

---

12. Bruce, *1 and 2 Thessalonians*, p. 12.

13. *The Epistles of Paul to the Romans and the Thessalonians*, p. 334.

14. See 3:12 in regard to love, 4:10 in regard to hope, and 4:12 and 5:18 in regard to faith, hope, and love.

15. Paul connects love to holiness in 3:12-13. My presumption is that, as Paul connects faith and hope to love (1:3), the idea of holiness summarizes living in faith, hope, and love.

the word of God, allowing it to work in them, believers also know suffering and so become imitators of the pillars of the faith — Christ, Paul and his coworkers (1:6), and the churches of Judea (2:14). Having faith and love (3:6) and suffering (3:3) are two sides of the same coin — together they create the currency of the life worthy of God.

Paul hopes for a time when this will not be the case, when faith, hope, and love will be expressed in the context of the coming of the Lord Jesus (3:12-13), when even death will be defeated and the faithful can live in peace forever with the Lord (4:17). The characteristics of faith, hope, and love, then, are signs of what *is to be*. Put another way, faith, hope, and love are the only dispositions that can protect from the coming wrath and that fit within God's kingdom and glory (2:12). As Paul says elsewhere, they will always be (1 Cor 13:13). In that sense, faith, hope, and love fit awkwardly in this time, for they properly belong to the time when God will set all things right. These graces belong to the coming kingdom.

In this time, faith, hope, and love are armor against the darkness (5:8), which means at the same time that they are targeted by the powers of darkness. The signs of light that are faith, hope, and love make those who exhibit these signs vulnerable to a dark and dangerous world. Nevertheless, these signs are critical to the deliverance strategy of God. Not only are they critical for the moment when Christ comes to complete God's salvation, but they are critical now. In effect, being holy in this time means that when the Lord Jesus comes he has somewhere to land. The Lord Jesus' coming descent (4:16) has a destination and purpose because there are people who have dedicated themselves to holiness. The Thessalonians' faith, hope, and love are essential for God's completion of God's saving project.

Their holiness in this time is always accompanied by affliction (3:4-6). To be being sanctified is to suffer. Furthermore, this mode of life of sanctification and suffering is one which aids God. Faith and love, Paul says, are tasks the believer undertakes in this time (1:3), tasks undertaken in the company of suffering. Together, believers' growth in holiness and the accompanying suffering create light in the nighttime of the present.

Recognizing the significance for God's work that believers should exercise faith, hope, and love and that these graces be exercised in a threatening arena (5:8) strengthens our earlier thought that the suffering of believers is necessary for God's salvific purposes.

TWO QUESTIONS ARISE, which we may ponder but which cannot be fully answered from the evidence in this brief letter. The first concerns the cause of believer-specific suffering, and the second concerns the relationship of the suffering of believers to their sanctification.

The Cause of Believer-Specific Suffering

As I have interpreted Paul's words to the Thessalonians, it appears that suffering is unavoidable; affliction is a certain attendant to belief in Christ. I have suggested that Paul understood the suffering of believers to be essential to God's rescue endeavor initiated in Jesus Christ. The question is, what is the cause of this suffering? Do believers suffer because they exhibit the characteristics of the kingdom in a world that is at odds with the kingdom? Do believers suffer as a result of being round pegs in a world that is full of square holes? That is, is there suffering that is specific to believers because the act of being a believer inherently alienates one from the rest of the world? Do believers suffer because they are children of light (1 Thess 5:5) in a time of night?

This is not a question Paul answers. However, in pondering this question we might notice that Paul goes out of his way to encourage his converts to be respected by those who do not believe in Jesus. Paul directs the Thessalonians to live quietly and not cause waves in their community so that they might live decently with "those outside" (4:12). That is, Paul specifically requests his converts to avoid provocative behavior and directs them instead to live in a way that draws the least attention to themselves, that causes the least offense.[16]

16. K. P. Donfried's suggestion that Paul co-opts political and social terms such as ἐκκλησία, παρουσία, ἀπάντησις, and κύριος ("The Assembly of the Thessalonians:

This would suggest that the suffering specific to believers does not come because believers force themselves on others or because they seek to draw attention to their alternative, even subversive, lifestyle. Believer-specific suffering, as it is discussed in 1 Thessalonians, must have some cause other than believers' own provocation.

On the other hand, it seems clear that while believers are not to advertise their distinctiveness, in Paul's view, they *are* different from "those outside." This difference is characterized by their commitment to the work of faith, the labor of love, and steadfastness in hope (1:3), which is the indication of their election (1:4). And faith, hope, and love are targets, since, in Paul's view, they indicate that those exhibiting them are destined to escape the coming wrath, "to obtain salvation through our Lord Jesus Christ" (5:8-9).

Paul declines, at least in this letter, to provide a theory or an explanation for the suffering specific to being a believer. What we can say on the basis of 1 Thessalonians is that those who are being saved draw to themselves arrows of pain. This is not because believers in Jesus are provocateurs. Rather, it is part of the odd tempo of this time of waiting for the coming of the Lord Jesus that those who live according to the beat of faith, hope, and love may come into conflict with those who do not.

Suffering for believers is, however, more than simply the result of being misfits in a particular age. Indications from this letter suggest that the suffering of believers contributes to the end of all suffering, for it is part of the painful process of bringing in the new age. By being people who exhibit the traits of the coming kingdom (2:12), believers in Jesus, perhaps inadvertently, announce the end of the age that is.

As the drama of Christ reveals, the mysterious dynamics of God's

---

Reflections on the Ecclesiology of the Earliest Christian Letter," in *Paul, Thessalonica, and Early Christianity* [Grand Rapids: Eerdmans, 2002], pp. 139-62, here p. 144) does not conflict with my interpretation. Paul may well be reshaping the Thessalonians' self-understanding so that they come to regard themselves as distinct from other assemblies in Thessalonica. At the same time, Paul cautions against his converts taking an offensive strategy on the grounds of their distinctiveness. They may be different, but they should act peaceably in their city.

cosmos are such that release from suffering requires suffering. Paul says that his converts undertake an affliction that imitates that of Christ (1:6). This appears to mean that believers' suffering is caused, as was Christ's, by acting for God's deliverance of God's creation from all that denies the love of God. Paul entreats his converts to remember and recognize what kind of people he and his coworkers proved themselves to be when they were first with the Thessalonians. What distinguished them, Paul says, is that they acted for the Thessalonians, that what they did was for the sake of the Thessalonians: "you know what kind of people we proved to be among you *for your sake*" (1:5). What the Thessalonians imitated in Paul and his company, and in the Lord, was a focus on others. The word they accepted was a word that directed them outside themselves. And this new direction was accompanied by joy as well as by affliction (1:6). Believer-specific suffering, then, is related to embracing care for the other in imitation of Christ and in reflection of God's own love (4:9).

Consequently, it is not simply that believers know affliction because we are foreigners in this age devoted to itself and not to God. Believers know affliction primarily because affliction is the necessary prelude to release, to the birth of the new age in which God's will is done. And believers, who are essential to God's continuing project of delivering God's creation from evil, will necessarily partake of suffering, since, as Christ himself demonstrated, deliverance requires suffering.

Suffering and Sanctification

In the course of considering the cause of believer-specific suffering we have contemplated how this suffering is related to God's saving intentions. Now we will consider the second question introduced above: do believers suffer *in order* to be sanctified?

The burden of this second question falls on the relation between believers' suffering and sanctification — is suffering necessary in order for believers to grow in holiness? Again, as with the first question, there are intimations rather than assertions in Paul's words to the Thessalonians. These intimations allow us only to create a cartoon and not the final portrait of Paul's understanding of suffering's relationship to sanctification.

Paul speaks of having been tested by God and of being in a state of being approved by God (2:4).[17] While he does not say that his testing and approval were the result of his suffering, he does speak of these things almost immediately following his statement that he and his coworkers had suffered and been mistreated at Philippi (2:2) and that at Thessalonica they had preached the gospel of God in the face of great opposition (2:2). It is, then, not much of a leap to suggest that this reference to Paul's capacity for struggle (ἀγών) is connected to God's testing of and approval of him. The athletic metaphor is a favorite of Paul's in referring to his own life in Christ (e.g., Phil 3:13-14).[18] This metaphor, of course, includes the idea of hard work and extension of oneself beyond the norm.[19] The relation of pain to gain is essential to the athletic metaphor. Paul's allusion to an athletic struggle in 1 Thess 2:2 suggests that he understood his approval by God to be connected to his own willingness to suffer for the sake of the gospel. Paul describes his life as like an athlete's, full of struggle as he strains toward God's call in Christ Jesus, a call which, coming from the Holy One, can be nothing except a call to holiness.

It appears, then, that Paul understood his willingness to suffer for the sake of the gospel of God as connected to his own sanctification. In 1 Thessalonians Paul connects his holy and righteous and blameless behavior to his willingness to extend himself beyond the norm for the sake of the Thessalonians (2:9-10). He sees his sanctity manifest in his capacity to accept hardship for the sake of others, thereby intimating that he may have interpreted his afflictions as necessary for his growth toward God.

If at the time of writing 1 Thessalonians Paul understood his own suffering as contributing positively to his increase in holiness, did he un-

---

17. Note that δοκιμάζω occurs in both the perfect passive and the present participial form in this verse.

18. See the important work by Pfitzner, *Paul and the Agon Motif.*

19. See Phil 3:13: ἐπεκτείνομαι.

derstand the suffering of other believers in the same way? There is little if any indication in 1 Thessalonians that he did. Paul does not draw a line between the Thessalonians' evident and current afflictions and their equally evident and current demonstration of holiness. Paul acknowledges his cherished converts' past (1:6; 2:14) and present (3:3-4) struggles and commends their past (1:7) and present (3:6; 4:9-10) holiness, but he does not connect the two. Perhaps at this stage of Paul's understanding he had not yet contemplated the role of suffering in sanctification for believers other than himself.

What Believer-Specific Suffering Is Not

What more we may say about the suffering believers undergo, as it is addressed in 1 Thessalonians, is primarily what it is not. Believer-specific suffering is not suffering that is sought for its own sake. It comes as an accompaniment to the main melody shaped by the dynamic, conviction-producing word of God. Even where there are indications that suffering contributes to sanctification, this suffering is neither an end in itself nor explicitly described as a means to a holy end. The relationship of suffering to sanctification is subtle and indirect. Affliction is the companion of the gospel in this time and so accompanies those who preach and live the gospel. The holiness that results from accepting the word of the gospel is then lived in the presence of suffering. While it does appear that Paul understood his own willingness to suffer for the gospel to have been commended by God, the important observation to keep in the forefront at this juncture is that suffering comes with belief in the gospel — it is, then, not something that the believer seeks. Suffering will rather find the believer. And, furthermore, while the affliction specific to believers appears to have some relation to sanctification (at least for Paul himself), that relation is not something the believer himself or herself controls or uses. It is simply a relationship that exists, and Paul in this letter leaves it at that. Holiness and suffering go together, but it is unclear exactly how.

Believer-specific suffering is also not all there is. Belief in the gospel is accompanied not only by affliction but also by joy (1:6). This is significant for our consideration of Paul's understanding of suffering since it means he understood believer-specific suffering to take place in the arena of joy. The quality of this suffering will then be affected by the fact that it takes place not in the bleakness of suffering alone but is rather infused with the colors of joy. And so Paul can pray for the safety of the Thessalonians' spirits, souls, and bodies during this tumultuous time before the parousia in the same breath as praying that the God of *peace* will sanctify them entirely (5:23). The dangers the Thessalonians experience now, in other words, are experienced in the arena of God's sanctifying activity. Their afflictions brew alongside joy (1:6) in the vast cauldron of God's peace and love.

The Thessalonians' imitation of Christ comes not only from the fact that the Thessalonians accepted affliction when they accepted the gospel but also from the fact that joy seasons their afflictions (1:6). It is this strange combination of suffering and joy that reveals that the Thessalonians, like Paul and his associates and like Christ before them, have received the word as it was meant to be received. Christ is the paradigmatic recipient of God's word. His acceptance of "the word" in suffering and with joy shapes the model to which those who believe in him may conform.

Suffering of Nonbelievers

The evidence from 1 Thessalonians is that for Paul there is a difference in both manner and kind between the sufferings of believers and that of nonbelievers. As I read the hints from 1 Thessalonians, Paul thought that one facet that distinguished believers' and nonbelievers' afflictions is the manner in which each suffers. Furthermore, Paul thinks that just as there are some sufferings that are peculiar to believers, so there is suffering specific to nonbelievers.

The first thing to notice about the matter of the suffering of nonbelievers in 1 Thessalonians is that there is so little about it. Paul is focused here almost entirely on his church in Thessalonica and their life of faith. When Paul does take his eyes off his treasured converts he does so primarily in order to emphasize for them how blessedly distinct they are from "the others."

There is, however, one significant passage related to the distinctive *manner* in which nonbelievers suffer. In the context of assuring the Thessalonians that even though some members of their assembly have died, Paul talks about how "the others" grieve because of death (4:13). Both believers and nonbelievers grieve in the face of death, but they do so in different ways. Believers grieve in hope, whereas, seen from the believers' perspective, nonbelievers grieve without hope. In contrast to some commentators who understand Paul to be directing his converts "not (to) sorrow at all,"[20] I interpret Paul's command not to grieve as the others do to be a directive about how the church *is* to grieve.

Moreover, as hope is one-third of the triad that includes faith and love (1:3), it is not stretching too far to suggest that Paul would regard nonbelievers facing other forms of suffering not only as without hope, but also as without faith and love. Furthermore, since Paul understands joy to be the special companion of the suffering believers know, nonbelievers suffer not only without the graces of faith, hope, and love but also without being able to know joy as they suffer.

As to the *kinds* of sufferings nonbelievers undergo, Paul refers to their experiencing God's coming wrath. In 1 Thessalonians Paul never states or implies that the unconverted are aware that there is an approaching day of wrath. In fact, he depicts unbelievers as being asleep and drunk (5:6-7), implying that they cannot see or understand what is about to befall them. The suffering they will know is, then, in the future and is even more pitiable and tragic because currently these "others" (5:6) are blind to what is about to hit them.[21]

---

20. Frame, p. 165.

21. I follow those in the commentary tradition, e.g., Frame (pp. 113-14), Bruce (p. 48), B. R. Gaventa (*First and Second Thessalonians* [Interpretation; Louisville: John Knox, 1998], pp. 37-38), who understand 2:16b ("God's wrath has come upon [the Judeans] εἰς τέλος") to refer not to what currently is but to what will be. Using language reminiscent of Jewish apocalyptic (e.g., *Testament of Levi* 6:11), Paul states that the Judeans' rejection of the gospel is a sign that they will not escape the coming wrath.

It should be noted that while Paul sees nonbelievers as consigned to the approaching wrath, he at the same time regards them as worthy of being loved. Paul encourages the Thessalonians to love not only other believers but "all people" (3:12). If Paul thought that unbelievers were destined for wrath, this did not mean that they were not to be loved.

Paul regards the Lord as the source of the love believers should have for nonbelievers (3:12), thereby indicating his understanding that the Lord loves all people. This strongly hints that Paul thought that the wrath awaiting those outside Christ is not what God would wish for them. Even though Paul writes a few lines (2:14-16) with the bite that comes from rejection, it bears emphasizing that Paul does not use nonbelievers' distinctive suffering as a warrant for believers to do anything other than follow God in loving these "others."

Summary

Paul regarded the suffering that attends belief in the gospel as anything but accidental — acceptance of the gospel is at the same time acceptance of suffering. In the case of the Thessalonians, gospel suffering included rejection by their neighbors. This particular form of suffering is rooted in the affliction that accompanies the word of the gospel — it is an affliction that imitates the affliction of Christ.

Just as Christ's afflictions were the vessel through which God's deliverance was borne, intimations from 1 Thessalonians are that Paul thought that believers' afflictions act also as a conduit for God's salvation. Furthermore, believers' faith, love, and hope, which are employed in the company of suffering, contribute to God's saving project. As suffering is the unavoidable companion of these graces, Paul appears to have thought of suffering as a necessary aspect of the current work of God.

Believer-specific suffering is not sought. It simply comes with accepting the gospel. In fact, Paul recommends that his converts do all they can to avoid confrontation with their neighbors and encourages them to love all people. Afflictions are the paradoxical attendants to the joyful good news, perhaps because, as just noted, they serve the purpose of continuing and completing God's saving work — a work which Christ demonstrated cannot take place apart from suffering. However, believer-specific suffering is undergone in a particular manner; it is experienced in concert with joy. And it is accompanied by faith, hope, and love.

Paul does not address whether, for believers other than himself, suffering contributes to growth in holiness. He appears to have thought that his own hardships in preaching the gospel brought him divine approval, but he does not relate the Thessalonians' sufferings to their commendable holiness.

There is next to nothing about the suffering of nonbelievers in 1 Thessalonians. What there is suggests that Paul thought that humanity apart from Christ suffered without either joy or the graces of faith, hope, and love. It would seem that Paul did not relish the thought of nonbelievers having to suffer in this fashion. His words in context indicate rather that he recognized, perhaps even empathized with, the desolation surrounding such a manner of suffering.

Paul mentions the impending wrath of God as the suffering that is specific to nonbelievers. Again, Paul's letter to the Thessalonians discourages an attitude of vengeance on the part of believers who may recognize this terrible end awaiting nonbelievers. Rather, Paul encourages believers to access and demonstrate the love God has for all people.

Using 1 Thessalonians to Talk about Suffering

Believer-Specific Suffering: The Challenge to Suffer

Paul claims, on the basis of the way Christ received the gospel, that the good news does not insulate believers from suffering. Rather, the good news is accompanied by an affliction peculiar to the gospel. This letter addresses the fact that by being believers, we are also sufferers. The suffering we will know is specific to being believers; it comes because we are imitating Christ. This letter serves to challenge complacent, fearful, and unaware Christians to accept gospel suffering. The good news Paul proclaimed was the good news Christ received and so it is uncomfortable. The task of believers is to imitate Christ's reception of the gospel, to turn in complete faith to God and to turn with God toward God's world with the desire only to participate in God's activity of healing and saving. As Christ's life shows, in the mysterious architecture of God's creation this desire for deliverance necessitates suffering.

Once this challenge is recognized, the first thing that must be said is that such suffering is unbidden. Believers are here not encouraged to provoke situations in order to know suffering. In fact, Paul exhorts quite the opposite manner of being in the world. Believers in Jesus Christ are to live quietly and command respect. Nevertheless, Paul is certain that there is suffering that attends faith in Christ. That is, Christians will suffer simply because they are Christians. In the apostle's time this suffering included persecution (2:14), perhaps even the killing of some of Paul's converts.[22]

The Reasons for Believer-Specific Suffering

This letter addresses the suffering that results from living a life of faithfulness to Christ. Thankfully, many North Atlantic Christians do not experience this suffering as physical persecution. Nevertheless, there are afflictions that come with the life of faith and this letter opens our eyes to that reality. Having our eyes open to this truth is important not only for the sheer value of being aware, but also because, by understanding the nature of the Christian life in regards to suffering, we should be able also to experience suffering's companion — joy.

Believers in Christ are, Paul says, people whose lives are shaped by

22. Donfried argues, following a suggestion by F. F. Bruce, that "the dead in Christ" (4:16) were killed during the persecutions in Thessalonica ("The Cults of Thessalonica and the Thessalonian Correspondence," in *Paul, Thessalonica, and Early Christianity,* pp. 41-43).

faith, by hope, and by love. These characteristics, these graces, are dynamic entities. They are more than dispositions in the sense of attitudes of mind. Faith, hope, and love are potent forces that believers work with and for. We work faith, we labor love, and we persevere in hope. The Christian life is a life devoted to increasing our connection with, our use of, our shaping by faith, hope, and love. These remarkable modes of life are aspects of God's life; they are aspects of holiness.

The peculiar situation of Christians is that the holy material we are privileged to work with is material that is perfectly fitted for the time of the *coming* of Christ. This holy material is, however, at odds with *this* time of darkness and of waiting for salvation. Faith, hope, and love properly belong not to the present nighttime but to the day (5:8). And so, those who exhibit these powerful forms of God's life will be embattled (5:8).

The suffering that is peculiar to the believer is, then, not suffering that results from forcing one's ways on others, not suffering that comes from trying to provoke, not suffering that is sought for its own sake. It is the suffering of misfits. Believers' energy is focused on participating in the energies of faith, hope, and love and these energies are out of tune with the dynamics of the present time.

The particular and individual ways that suffering will attend the working with and for faith, hope, and love are not outlined in this letter, nor could they be. Presumably, the cost of exercising these graces will be different for each believer and each group of believers. What is helpful for us to take from this letter is that employing faith, hope, and love will put us at odds with those Paul characterizes as on the look-out for "peace and security" (5:3) in all the wrong places.

The choice to exercise faith when the most reasonable and obvious option is suspicion and self-defense;[23] the choice to labor in love when the most expedient course of action is attack or use of social power or

---

23. We must be cautious about using this letter to encourage any type of victimization. The simple fact of Paul's energetic, athletic rhetoric when speaking of his own afflictions in imitation of Christ blocks any attempt to manipulate this text to endorse victimhood or victimization.

exclusion of people or groups who offend;[24] the choice to persevere in hope when it seems clear that the enemy's lines are drawn, that the die is cast, that disease or loss has had the last word — these choices make fools of believers in a world that values the peace and security that can be garnered from this time. And such folly will not survive unscathed.

The efforts of faith, love, and hope will result in bruises received from those without and within the Christian faith. And, of course, we will all, at one time or another, be those who are offended by or misunderstand others' exercise of these graces.

1 Thessalonians challenges us to notice where we subtly, and perhaps overtly, avoid exercising our option to work faith, to labor love, and to be steadfast in hope. This letter challenges us to ask ourselves whether we avoid putting our energies into these modes of life because we recognize at some level that to do so will be costly.

Our Suffering Is Productive

If we allow ourselves to see that Christ is the paradigm for how we are to receive the gospel, we may interpret the difficulties that will come from exercising faith, hope, and love as productive conflicts. In this time of waiting (1:10), by working with faith, hope, and love, we work with the defining features of Christ. We are, like Christ, working for the deliverance of this age from the dreadful grip of night. Directing our energies to faith, hope, and love is to participate in God's project of deliverance.

This grand vision may be hard to hold onto in the moment-by-moment decisions involved in making choices for faith, hope, and love. Paul's words encourage us to see both that our efforts are part of God's current saving work and that our efforts, while costly, will be rewarded. Paul is convinced that the reward far outweighs whatever troubles will necessarily attend our exercising faith, love, and hope. The reward of

24. Calvin speaks of "how burdensome love is" (*The Epistles of Paul to the Romans and the Thessalonians*, p. 335).

acting in imitation of Christ in this time is that in the future we will be able to live with him forever (5:10). Furthermore, Paul hints that courageous and energetic commitment to the gospel in the face of opposition is approved by God and works to create holiness in the believer.

Accepting the challenge to suffer will allow us to grow into the likeness of the one who is holy and righteous and blameless.

Our appointment to suffering has also other benefits. For our attention to faith, hope, and love means that when we experience the trials of this age we can respond from the resources of the time that is to come — a time when there will be no suffering for believers. Consequently, when believers face, for instance, the death of loved ones, we can grieve in hope.

Joy

Paul's words also clarify that the present reward of belief in Jesus Christ, which is joy, can be known only as we accept the gospel in affliction. Joy springs not from a pain-free environment but from suffering. It is as we suffer in this time in imitation of the Lord that we will know the joy that he also knew.

It must be emphasized that the rewards for gospel suffering just mentioned are awarded not because we seek suffering for its own sake but because we receive the gospel in imitation of the way Christ received it. The difference is essential. If we seek suffering in order to gain rewards our focus is on ourselves. If we receive the gospel in a manner that imitates Christ, our focus is on Christ and so it will be on God and God's creation.

The outward focus that characterized Christ's reception of the word, and Paul's, is paradoxically both the cause of suffering and the cause of joy. In other words, suffering sought for oneself, in order to control or quicken one's growth in holiness, will not be accompanied by the Spirit's joy. Suffering that comes because it is the strange companion of the good news, which is received and enacted with eyes turned toward others, will know another friend — the joy of the Holy Spirit.

Suffering and Sanctification

The challenge to suffer is to be kept separate from the desire for sanctification. We cannot create our own holiness, even though we must labor in faith, love, and hope. Our lives of focus on God and others through faith, love, and hope will be pierced with affliction, but how that affliction shapes us into holy people is not under our control. The challenge to suffer is, then, not a call to seek out suffering. It is rather an exhortation to continue in faith, love, and hope while we suffer. It is an encouragement to see that this uncomfortable mixture of graces and pain is, through God's grace, producing deliverance for us and for God's creation.

The Suffering of Nonbelievers

As we have seen, despite the fact that Paul's reference to the Thessalonians' sufferings (2:14) has a vengeful tone, this tone is sounded only once.[25] The main approach Paul takes toward nonbelievers is one of respect, indeed, of care. We might distinguish between Paul's attitude to those who persecute and hinder believers and those who do not know Christ. His condemnation, of course, is reserved for the former.

Paul's words concerning those who do not know about Christ might suggest a rather detached, judgmental response to nonbelievers — they are unaware that their misguided trust in this world's "peace and security" means that "sudden destruction" awaits them (5:2). Paul's actions, however, suggest another response. His actions demonstrate his profound care for those who do not know about Christ; after all, he risked his life to preach the gospel. And, as we have seen, something of what I understand as his compassion toward those not graced with hope peeks through when Paul refers to their grief at the death of loved ones (4:13).

---

25. We note that in none of the other references to his affliction or that of other believers does Paul also excoriate those causing the pain.

Making Paul's Response to Nonbelievers Our Own

Paul understands love as the godly response to all people (3:12). When we experience hatred from those who reject the gospel, we may choose to recognize our bitter hurt, but then move toward the place where joy finds us again. Moreover, Paul may encourage us, from the resource afforded by the potent mixture of affliction and joy, to grow, indeed, to use his lovely word, to "abound," in love toward all people. Paul's response may season that of the rest of us so that we regard the suffering of nonbelievers as nothing other than a cause for our compassion and action.

3

PHILIPPIANS

Assurance in Suffering

～～～

Paul wrote the letter that came to be known as Philippians while he was in chains. While this incarceration clearly allowed him enough freedom to send letters, to receive aid and news, and to continue to direct his coworkers in matters related to his mission,[1] he was in prison, a place designed to create enormous discomfort.[2] Paul suffers as he writes this letter. There are some who read Paul as "the Stoic sage" and hear his words as indicating that "he is anything but pained."[3] This acoustics for reading Paul's letter to Philippi is different from mine and many others in the long tradition of the church.[4] As will be seen, my

1. See 2:19-25, where Paul records directions involving Timothy and Epaphroditus.

2. Cf. S. Fowl: "the manifestly gruesome conditions of imperial prisons induced despair in virtually all those subjected to them" ("Believing Forms Seeing: Formation for Martyrdom in Philippians," in *Character and Scripture: Moral Formation, Community, and Biblical Interpretation*, ed. W. P. Brown [Grand Rapids: Eerdmans, 2002], pp. 317-30, here p. 320). See B. Rapske, *The Book of Acts in Its First Century Setting* III: *The Book of Acts and Paul in Roman Custody* (Grand Rapids: Eerdmans, 1994); C. S. Wansink, *Chained in Christ: The Experience and Rhetoric of Paul's Imprisonments* (Journal for the Study of the New Testament Supplement Series 130; Sheffield: Sheffield Academic, 1996).

3. T. Engberg-Pederson, *Paul and the Stoics* (Edinburgh: Clark, 2000), p. 98.

4. For a selective and intelligent, though brief, overview of Christian thinkers from Ignatius of Antioch to J. B. Lightfoot and J. T. Forestell who have heard suffering

view is that the tapestry of Philippians is strung with references to suffering: the suffering of Paul, the suffering of Christ, and the suffering of the Philippians.[5] The red thread of suffering trails across the pages of this letter.[6]

Suffering as a Believer

Philippians provides us with a firsthand account of a believer in Christ who is suffering. It would appear that, due to the circumstances of his

---

in Paul's Philippian words, see L. G. Bloomquist, *The Function of Suffering in Philippians* (Sheffield: JSOT, 1993), pp. 18-34.

5. I am not claiming that the web of suffering references provides a clue to the long-standing scholarly question of the letter's integrity. That is another question for another time. I will work with canonical Philippians, leaving the question aside of whether or not it is a composite letter. I do, however, agree with M. Bockmuehl and others that "partition theories . . . raise more questions than they answer" (*The Epistle to the Philippians* [Black's New Testament Commentaries; London: Black, 1997], p. 25). For a record of some of the more substantial arguments for and against the integrity of Philippians, see L. A. Jervis, *The Purpose of Romans: A Comparative Letter Structure Investigation* (Journal for the Study of the New Testament Supplement Series 55; Sheffield: Sheffield Academic, 1991), pp. 65-68; P. T. O'Brien, *The Epistle to the Philippians* (New International Greek Testament Commentary; Grand Rapids: Eerdmans, 1991), pp. 10-18; Wansink, p. 96, n. 2.

Bloomquist analyzes the critical role reference to suffering plays in the rhetorical and epistolary shape of Philippians. One way my study differs from Bloomquist's is in not working overtly with the disciplines of rhetoric or epistolography. It coincides with his work, however, in reckoning with the central role that the theme of suffering plays in Philippians.

6. P. S. Minear's examination of the Philippian hymn pays homage to E. Lohmeyer's conviction (*Die Briefe an die Philipper, and die Kolosser und an Philemon* [Göttingen: Vandenhoeck und Ruprecht, 1953]) that the chief issue in Philippians was the threat of martyrdom for both Paul and the church. Minear, as do I, queries whether the letter is as laden with references to martyrdom as Lohmeyer proposed. Nevertheless, Minear rightly recognizes that this letter is steeped in suffering ("Singing and Suffering in Philippi," in *The Conversation Continues: Studies in Paul and John in Honor of J. Louis Martyn*, ed. R. T. Fortna and B. R. Gaventa [Nashville: Abingdon, 1990], pp. 202-19, here p. 218). (Minear and I part company, as will be seen, on the matter of whether the suffering that suffuses this letter is understood by Paul as persecution.)

imprisonment, Paul reflected on suffering in a manner that was much broader and deeper than we have so far encountered through our study of 1 Thessalonians. While it may sound callous, it must be said that Paul's pain was for our gain, for in this letter we find astonishing meditations on the organic connections between Christ's suffering and Paul's own[7] and on the wondrous rewards of participation in such suffering. Paul's pain is also our pain, since Paul is convinced that suffering is a part of a believer's life.

In Philippians we are allowed insight into a new stage of Paul's life of faith.[8] He has learned some things in the course of his relationship with Jesus Christ (4:11). His hardships have both encouraged him to be forward-looking (3:12-14) and stimulated him to deep reflections on the trials and hopes of living "in Christ." Whereas in 1 Thessalonians Paul evidences an *acceptance* that the good news is accompanied by affliction, by the time he writes Philippians he is motivated to reflect on the *value* of suffering as a believer. It is no accident that it is in writing Philippians that Paul uses the powerful and provocative hymn extolling the good outcome of Christ's humiliation, suffering, and death (2:5-11).[9]

Unlike 1 Thessalonians, where in the opening thanksgiving Paul recognizes the affliction of his converts, in Philippians Paul initially features his own sufferings. The prominence that the role of his afflictions takes in this letter is due not only to the fact that he mentions them in the first instance but also to the fact that, even after proceeding to highlight Christ's sufferings (2:6-8), Paul returns to a reflection on his own afflictions, this time relating them directly to Christ's (3:7-10). Paul, that

---

7. Minear beautifully elucidates the correlation that Paul draws in Philippians between his own experience of humiliation and that of Christ ("Singing and Suffering in Philippi," pp. 205-7).

8. Cf. R. Cassidy, *Paul in Chains: Roman Imprisonment and the Letters of St. Paul* (New York: Crossroad, 2001), p. 188.

9. See especially R. P. Martin for discussion of Phil 2:5-11 as an early Christian hymn incorporated by Paul into his Philippian letter (*Carmen Christi: Philippians ii.5-11 in Recent Interpretation and in the Setting of Early Christian Worship* [Grand Rapids: Eerdmans, 1983; reprint of 1967 with new preface]). The discovery of this as a hymn is usually credited to E. Lohmeyer, *Kyrios Jesus* (Heidelberg: Winter, 1928); idem, *Die Briefe.*

is, brackets his description of Christ's paradigmatic sufferings almost exclusively with reference to his own.

Paul's difficulties at the time of writing Philippians are substantial. He does not describe his circumstances simply as imprisonment. He speaks rather of being in fetters.[10] That these chains were less than comfortable is indicated both by his repeated reference to them (1:7, 13, 14, 17) and by his accusation that some are trying to add pressure to them (1:17)[11] — the implication being that they already are a source of pain. Chains in imprisonment were not only a way to prevent escape. The very weight of chains was part of a prisoner's punishment. At times the weight was so great that arms and legs were permanently disfigured or disabled.[12]

Paul's bound and painful state may also account for the letter's abundance of athletic references.[13] The limitations and discomforts of his body in all likelihood focused Paul's mind at once on the capacities of his body and on how the same energy that is required for the athletic struggle must be applied to living life "in Christ."

Likewise, Paul's description of the present state of his and others' bodies as "humble" (3:21), a word he contrasts with abundance (4:12) and elsewhere connects with suffering and death (2:8), hints at the difficult circumstances he is in as he writes this letter. His hope for a glorious body like Christ's glorious risen body (3:21) again suggests that at present Paul is experiencing bodily torment from which he hopes for release. There is, of course, nothing that directs attention to the body so much as pain. Likewise, Paul's conviction that the good news is good also for our physical bodies (1:20; 3:21) suggests his current discomfort.

---

10. The NRSV translation "my imprisonment" (1:7) masks the actual Greek word δεσμός (chains, bonds, fetters). As G. D. Fee notes, while "chains" might be a metonym for imprisonment, it is most likely that Paul was actually chained, perhaps to his guards (*Paul's Letter to the Philippians* [New International Commentary on the New Testament; Grand Rapids: Eerdmans, 1995], p. 92).

11. So J. B. Lightfoot, who sees here a metaphorical use of θλίψις, where Paul plays with the word's literal meaning of "pressure" or "friction" (*St. Paul's Epistle to the Philippians* [Peabody: Hendrickson, 1987, reprint of 1868], p. 90).

12. See Rapske, *The Book of Acts and Paul in Roman Custody*, p. 208.

13. 1:27, 30; 2:16; 3:12-14; 4:3; perhaps also 2:12.

Not only is Paul hurting in body, he also knows mental anguish. While he is bound in chains some people are preaching Christ insincerely, probably using the fact of his imprisonment for their own advantage and to discredit his message (1:15-17).[14] The brave front Paul attempts with his words "What then? Only that in every way, whether in pretense, or in truth, Christ is proclaimed; and in that I rejoice" (1:18) barely masks his immediately preceding admission that such action has the capacity to afflict him (1:17). Moreover, Paul hints at his worry that his imprisonment has taken the wind out of the sails of some believers. When he writes that *"most* of the brothers have been made confident in the Lord" because of his chains (1:14), Paul acknowledges that some do find his imprisonment a threat to their faith in Christ.

In the midst of these daunting afflictions Paul records among his most astonishing and profound thoughts regarding suffering. His provocative perspective is that Christ and suffering go hand in hand. This is something he already knew when he wrote 1 Thessalonians, but his understanding has now become richer and his articulation of this aspect of the faith more pronounced. Paul asserts that Christ strengthens him for all circumstances. In other words, Christ does not make Paul's difficulties disappear, but rather fortifies him to endure them.[15]

14. While admittedly going against the grain of New Testament scholarly consensus, it is worth pondering whether the others who are preaching Christ out of envy and on account of strife (1:15) are nonbelievers, perhaps even Paul's jailers. It is not beyond imagining that Paul's guards, recognizing that he is not afraid of them because he understands his suffering as being "in Christ" (see below), responded to this dazzling power shift by proclaiming Christ in order to mock the gospel on the basis of its proponent's humiliating condition.

15. τῷ ἐνδυναμοῦντι (4:13) refers to Christ; so, e.g., M. Silva, *Philippians* (Wycliffe Exegetical Commentary; Chicago: Moody, 1988), p. 236; F. W. Beare, *The Epistle to the Philippians* (Black's New Testament Commentaries; London: Black, 1969), p. 153; O'Brien, p. 527.

Philippians as an Apology for Suffering

The Challenge of Interpretation

Philippians, written by a believer in Jesus Christ, is an apology for suffering, and this in two ways. First and primarily, it is an apology or defense of Paul's own suffering. Second, it is an encouragement to other believers to accept afflictions while being "in" Christ. This is not to say, as E. Lohmeyer suggested, that Paul is concerned to promote martyrdom.[16] I rather suggest that the suffering Paul discusses is, as it were, of a more pedestrian variety.[17] Paul in Philippians is both contemplating suffering *while* believing and suffering *caused by* belief.

We will see that in Romans Paul has a more highly developed understanding. There, as I read him, Paul views believers' suffering as both "in Christ" and "with Christ." Believers inevitably experience the difficulties of human life, which they share with every person, but may do so "in Christ." Enduring difficulties (of whatever sort) while being a believer is what I term suffering *"in Christ."*

As well, believers experience suffering as a *result* of incorporation into Christ. This involves sharing Christ's sufferings and suffering for Christ's sake. These sufferings *"with Christ"* are in addition to the difficulties believers undergo along with all humanity. Suffering "with Christ" is an unavoidable aspect of being "in Christ"; suffering "with Christ," as Paul understands it in Romans (the germs of which understanding we have seen in 1 Thessalonians), involves resisting all injustices, claiming the hope that glory will swallow up suffering, and allow-

---

16. *Die Briefe an die Philipper.* See the critique of Lohmeyer in O'Brien, p. 70.

17. *Contra* Fowl, who sees Paul in Philippians concerned to shape his converts into people capable of understanding their potential deaths at the hands of people hostile to their faith "as willed offerings of themselves to God" ("Believing Forms Seeing," p. 330); also *contra* P. Perkins, who regards Philippians as an apology concerned with "the need to understand the social situation of the Christian community in the Greco-Roman *polis* in light of the persistent fact of persecution" ("Philippians: Theology for the Heavenly Politeuma," in *Pauline Theology*, ed. J. M. Bassler [Minneapolis: Fortress, 1991], I, pp. 89-104, here p. 92).

ing ourselves to be conformed to Christ. This suffering is on behalf of God's creation in both its human and non-human form.

In Philippians, however, Paul does not see things this clearly. Or, rather, here he simply holds together suffering while being "in Christ" with sharing Christ's suffering (suffering "with Christ").

This adds to the challenge of interpretation. It would be less than accurate (as many commentators have done) to regard Paul as describing or even advocating only what I have called suffering "with Christ" — suffering caused by belief in Christ, suffering that accrues only to believers. He also holds ideas about suffering "in Christ" — experiencing the difficulties of life in the context of Christ. Words like "that I . . . may share [Christ's] sufferings" (Phil 3:10) describe a believer-specific suffering. However, these words do not delimit Paul's meaning elsewhere in the letter.

When Paul speaks of his situation in prison he does not characterize it as persecution. Clearly, he is in prison because of his preaching Christ, but he does not identify his situation as one of suffering "with Christ" or for Christ's sake (despite usual English translations of 1:13). He rather simply says that he sees his difficult circumstances (as do others) as undergone "in Christ" (1:13). Here, unlike his reflections later in the letter (3:10), Paul is not concerned to extol the benefit of suffering caused by belief in Christ. He is rather reckoning with a situation of enduring afflictions in the special environment of being "in Christ." That is, in 1:13 Paul is not speaking of the cause of his sufferings.

Paul's thoughts on suffering are less defined in Philippians than they become in Romans, both in terms of the distinction between suffering *as* a believer and suffering *because* one is a believer and in terms of the character of each kind of suffering. For instance, when in Philippians Paul does meditate on suffering "with" (3:10), as opposed to "in" Christ (1:13), his thoughts lack the edge they have in Romans. In his letter to Rome, as we shall see, suffering "with Christ" contributes to God's redemptive movements for all creation. In Philippians, on the other hand, Paul sees sharing Christ's sufferings as having value for his own life (that "I may attain resurrection from the dead," 3:11), but not for anything beyond that.

The interpreter is, then, challenged to be true to the faint boundaries between Paul's talk of sufferings that result from belief in Christ and his talk of believers' sufferings as being experienced, like all of our lives, "in Christ." A sharp-edged approach that would (for the purpose of examination) cut loose either one or the other discourse about suffering in Philippians (as I will do in Romans) threatens to damage the delicate forms of Paul's reflections in his letter to Philippi. Likewise, it is an interpreter's responsibility not to fill in the shapes of Paul's thought so that they may look more solid than his words actually allow.

There is an ambiguity to Paul's thinking about suffering in Philippians because he holds together both the experience of suffering *because* he is a believer and suffering *as* a believer. In what follows, in order to be true to this ambiguity, I try to describe what Paul says without using the heuristic categories ("in Christ" and "with Christ" suffering) which will become useful when we turn to Romans.

The Reason for Paul's Apology

Before proceeding to demonstrate my view of Philippians as an apology for suffering we may note one of the implications of such a view. If Paul is attempting to defend his suffering to his own converts, then they must have been distressed on account of his circumstances. This approach to the letter is confirmed by the tone of his defense, which is declamatory rather than comforting.[18] Paul is at pains not so much to assure the Philippians that all is well as to acknowledge his afflictions and address their significance.[19] His words appear, then, to be directed to people

18. This is not the standard reading. D. E. Garland represents a more typical way of hearing Paul's tone: "Paul writes to those who were anxious about his situation . . . [he] attempts to inform and reassure his friends about" the meaning of his imprisonment ("Phil 1:1-26: The Defense and Confirmation of the Gospel," *Review and Expositor* 77 [1980]: 327-36, here p. 331). It is to be noted, however, that Paul's proof that his imprisonment is "for the defense of the gospel" (1:16) does not employ the language of affection.

19. Much current thinking on the epistolary form of Philippians regards it as a "letter of friendship." One of the planks in the argument is that Paul opens the letter-body with words of "reassurance" (so L. Alexander, "Hellenistic Letter-Forms and the Structure of Philippians," *Journal for the Study of the New Testament* 37 [1989]: 87-101, here

who, though worried about his welfare, are chiefly concerned about the seeming paradox of a suffering preacher of resurrection.[20] At the heart of Paul's response, and presumably of the Philippians' concern, is the fact that, for believers in the risen Christ, suffering continues.[21]

Paul's Defense

Paul's eagerness to defend his difficult circumstances surfaces early in this missive. After thanking God for his addressees (1:3-11), as he does in almost every letter, Paul tells his readers that he wants them to know that what has happened to him has resulted in the advancement of the gospel (1:12). Paul's words barely mask his self-defensive tone. And almost immediately the reason for his apology regarding his circumstances becomes clear: some are using his imprisonment as an opportunity to hurt his mission (1:15, 17). The letter strongly hints, then, that the fact of his imprisonment is being used to discredit his gospel.

---

p. 95). My view calls this into question. See Bockmuehl, pp. 34-35, for other reasons to be cautious about categorizing Philippians as a "letter of friendship." S. Stowers' proposal that Philippians is a "*hortatory* letter of friendship" (emphasis added) is closer to the mark. Stowers writes: "Paul must . . . convince his friends and enemies that his misfortune is, in reality, good fortune" ("Friends and Enemies in the Politics of Heaven: Reading Theology in Philippians," in *Pauline Theology*, I, pp. 105-22, here p. 114).

20. That Paul attacks the value of circumcision by extolling his suffering (3:2-10), for instance, is one of the features of the letter suggesting that the Philippians are puzzled, even provoked, by Paul's present afflictions. Paul's curious response in Philippians to the threat of the circumcisers (cf. his response in Galatians) strongly suggests that the promoters of circumcision were using Paul's sorry state to mock his version of the gospel. Perhaps they were offering, and his converts were willing to buy, circumcision as a defense against or antidote to suffering. Cf. Perkins, p. 102.

21. Like much in scholarship on Philippians, the question of why Paul wrote this letter has had a cornucopia of answers. My study is not concerned with the occasion of Philippians per se, but it may contribute to the mix. This mix already, of course, includes ideas similar to mine. For instance, in the course of making his proposal that Paul in Philippians is seeking to encourage his readers to have critical distance on the Roman authorities, Cassidy comments that some of Paul's readers were worried about their own fate (*Paul in Chains*, p. 188).

Paul seeks to deal with this situation by distinguishing between those who love him and those who do not. Those who love him, Paul writes, recognize that his situation is consonant with the gospel and for the sake of the gospel (1:16). Paul's accusation is: it is those who do not love him who have an incorrect interpretation of his incarceration. We may readily surmise that the fact of Paul's imprisonment was being used to claim that he and his gospel were disreputable. Calvin puts it: "those bad workmen . . . did not refrain from triumphing over the calamity of the holy man, and so making his Gospel contemptible."[22]

The relationship is unclear between those who do not love Paul and are preaching Christ, those whom Paul calls "dogs" (3:2), and the "enemies of the cross of Christ" (3:18).[23] Whether there are two or more groups at odds with Paul and his gospel or only one, the indications are that, as a consequence of these people, Paul feels obliged to make a defense in behalf of his miserable state. Moreover, although his particular suffering seems to be the primary target, it is not just his situation that is problematic. It is also the very fact of suffering in light of the good news that is at issue. And so, whether we read the reference to "enemies of the cross of Christ" (3:18) in conjunction with Paul's earlier reference to evil-doers who wish to mutilate the flesh (3:2)[24] or read it

22. *The Epistles of Paul the Apostle to the Galatians, Ephesians, Philippians and Colossians,* tr. T. H. L. Parker (Calvin's Commentaries; Grand Rapids: Eerdmans, 1965), p. 234. Cf. R. Jewett: Paul "was being charged with jeopardizing the mission by exhibiting a humility and suffering which were incompatible with the life of a Christian apostle" ("Conflicting Movements in the Early Church as Reflected in Philippians," *Novum Testamentum* 12 [1970]: 362-90, here p. 368).

23. For various opinions, see commentaries and D. K. Williams, *Enemies of the Cross of Christ: The Terminology of the Cross and Conflict in Philippians* (Journal for the Study of the New Testament Supplement Series 223; Sheffield: Sheffield Academic, 2002), esp. pp. 54-60.

24. In general terms, scholars like J. Gnilka ("Die Antipaulinische Mission in Philippi," *Biblische Zeitschrift* 9 [1965]: 258-76); J. Müller-Bardoff ("Zur Frage der literarischen Einheit des Philipperbriefes," *Wissenschaftlich Zeitschrift der Universetät Jena* 7 [1957-58]: 591-604); A. J. F. Klijn ("Paul's Opponents in Philippians iii," *Novum Testamentum* 7 [1965]: 278-84); and G. F. Hawthorne (*Philippians* [Word Biblical Commentary 43; Waco: Word, 1983], pp. xliv-xlvii) agree that the divide between Paul and

separately,[25] the point should not be lost that Paul's complaint in 3:18 concerns not these people's beliefs so much as their way of life. The way they "walk" (περιπατοῦσιν) is what is at issue for Paul.[26] His further description of them as people who "make their belly their god" (3:19) strongly hints that, in his view, discomfort is anathema for these people. And his accusation that they set their minds on "earthly things" is additional evidence that the threat that concerns Paul (whether or not these people are concerned also to create circumcised and Torah-observant Gentile believers in Christ) is behavior that would eschew suffering,[27] a condition he diagnoses as stemming from hating the cross.

As the only other mention of the cross in Philippians is in the highlight of the letter — the hymn of 2:6-11 — where Paul identifies Christ's cross with humility and death (2:8), the way of life Paul scorns is one that seeks to avoid suffering. His problem is with a lifestyle that avoids pain, just as presumably their problem was with a way of life willing to encounter it. Paul's emotional language betrays the threat he feels from such a disposition. These people may have had some similarities to the Corinthians whom Paul castigates for thinking themselves already kings, already filled, already rich (1 Cor 4:8), already raised (1 Cor 15:12).[28] The good news then (as now) was received by some as news about the resurrection alone, news that discounted, discredited, or denied the cross. The gospel was seen as an offer of happiness, capable of canceling out all trouble and pain; the practical result of the good news allowing believers to walk pain-free, engaging in the delights of cre-

---

his one set of opponents concerns the role of circumcision and Torah observance and the significance of the cross for righteousness.

25. See, for example, the commentaries of J. B. Lightfoot, pp. 154-55; F. F. Bruce, *Philippians* (San Francisco: Harper and Row, 1983), pp. 104-5; and Beare, pp. 133-34, where the reference in 3:2-6 is seen as directed toward a group with a Jewish agenda and the reference in 3:18-19 to another group, perhaps one with Gnostic or antinomian motivations.

26. Noted also by Fee, pp. 367-68.

27. So also O'Brien: "they were not prepared to participate in Christ's sufferings" (p. 454).

28. Cf. Minear, "Singing and Suffering in Philippi," p. 209.

ation ("earthly things"). Faced with the suffering of one who preached the good news, these people's response was confusion or contempt, for the very idea of suffering's presence in light of the gospel was for them problematic. Paul must, then, stake his defense on the continuing presence of the cross.

Paul's Suffering Is "In" Christ

Whatever the exact historical circumstances and personages motivating Paul's apology, it is clear that defending his imprisonment is a high priority for Paul. He opens the body of this letter with his defense,[29] claiming that the whole praetorian guard and "all the rest" have come to see that his chains are "in Christ" (1:13). This is usually interpreted to mean either that it is clear to his jailers that he is there because he is a Christian[30] or that they and others (whoever "all the rest" are, we do not know) are being, perhaps successfully, evangelized by Paul.[31] What Paul says, however, is simply that he suffers "in Christ."[32]

The distinction is critical. Reckoning his imprisonment as being "in Christ" strongly suggests that Paul is not pointing a finger at anyone. That is, *Paul is not interpreting his situation as one of persecution* — his imprisonment may be caused by his commitment to the gospel, but he chooses to interpret and present his situation from a deeper level. His suffering is not shaped by his jailers but by Christ.[33]

---

29. A Pauline letter typically begins with a salutation and then a thanksgiving before it proceeds to what is termed the opening of the letter body, in which the writer begins to introduce the issues that occasioned the letter.

30. So Beare, p. 57.

31. So Garland, p. 331.

32. Cf. Fee, p. 113.

33. If my reading of Paul's meaning is correct, and if such a meaning were indeed communicated (either implicitly or explicitly) to his jailers, the response of the praetorian guards to Paul's opinion may have ranged from anger, to admiration, and perhaps even to conversion. Perhaps Paul's direction to his converts to strive together for the faith of the gospel and not be frightened in anything by opponents since this is a sign of their salvation and of their opponents' destruction (1:27-28) reflects something Paul was experiencing. Indeed, if Paul's perspective on his situation reflects something other

In thus accepting his suffering, Paul does not accept victimization. He speaks rather as someone who has radically reversed the power dynamics of his circumstances. He is not the victim. Paul interprets the injustices he experiences in the context of being "in" Christ; other people and circumstances may cause afflictions, but Paul does not lay blame. He rather uses his energy to draw these difficulties into the sphere he now inhabits — the sphere of being "in" Christ. This is critical for Paul's defense of his present humiliation. For, his chief point is that being "in" Christ does not separate the believer from suffering. Paul stakes his defense on the continuing presence of the cross.

The Positive Effects of His Suffering

Paul claims that the manifestation of his chains as being "in Christ" is for the purpose of the progress of the gospel (1:13-14). The agent making it visible to "the whole praetorian guard and all the rest" is not named, but we may take it that Paul would credit God with this remarkable feat.[34] Paul's jailers and others have, he says, come to see more and more about the gospel because he is in chains.[35] He is asserting that those who keep him bound have witnessed the productive power of the gospel. They have, in other words, seen firsthand that the gospel redefines the connection between what is good and what is not. The good news Paul preaches can live in suffering; the power of the gospel, the power of being "in Christ," is that the most hostile and shameful circumstances are somehow incorporated into Christ. The good news does not separate or protect; it frees the believer from fear (1:28). All is in Christ. This paradoxical and profound understanding is, Paul claims, being increasingly understood by those who imprison him. They see, in other words, that though he is in chains, he is free, and this

---

than his own hope, he would be stating the astonishing fact that the praetorian guards themselves have come to see that being chained in Christ confirms the gospel rather than discrediting it.

34. Cf. Fowl, "Believing Forms Seeing," p. 320.

35. The word προκοπή (1:12) means progress toward a goal.

has helped the advance of the good news. This assertion, along with the next, serves to put meat on Paul's defense of his imprisonment.

Paul also claims that the manifestation of his chains as being "in Christ" has had a very positive effect on "most of the brothers" (1:14). They have been made confident in the Lord, resulting in greater boldness in proclamation and lack of fear in doing so. These claims contribute to Paul's defense of his suffering: there are some who do not recoil and are in fact emboldened by recognizing that Paul is suffering "in Christ."

Paul's conviction that it has been made visible that his fetters are "in Christ" is obviously ostensibly outrageous. And so Paul says that in order to recognize the reality of his situation, love is required. It is those who love who understand correctly that his chains are "in Christ" and that his very suffering is an ἀπολογία for the gospel (1:16). Love alone can know what is true about his suffering. This may be one of the reasons why Paul's prayer for the Philippians includes his desire that their "love may abound more and more, with all knowledge and discernment" (1:9).[36]

Gaining Christ Means Accepting Suffering

Christ is the lens through which Paul now views and experiences his situation. It is through Christ that Paul sees that all the security he had as a Hebrew of the Hebrews is actually only a liability (3:7). In fact, Christ initiated (δι' ὃν τὰ πάντα ἐζημιώθην, 3:8) the loss of all Paul had.[37] Though such radical loss took place, it strangely resulted in a gain — the gain of Christ and of being found "in him."

The purpose clause in 3:8b-9 — "in order that I might gain Christ

---

36. It is interesting to note in passing that Augustine, while not referring to Paul's words here, agrees with Paul on the capacity of love to allow believers understanding. In the context of a sermon encouraging recognition of Christ's divinity, Augustine writes: "Let your love apprehend this; attend ye to the great mystery" (*Sermon* 38, in *The Nicene and Post-Nicene Fathers* [Grand Rapids: Eerdmans, reprint], VI, p. 383).

37. My translation of 3:8b is: "through whom all things were forfeited"; that is, Paul signals Christ's agency in this forfeiture. We see a similar thought at 3:12, where Paul says he has been seized by Christ (κατελήμφθην ὑπὸ Χριστοῦ).

and be found in him" — speaks of both the future and the present.[38] Paul expresses here both his long-range goal and his current circumstances. When Christ effected Paul's loss of everything, Paul was not left in exile but was embraced by Christ. Paul's resultant condition is stable but not static. He will continue to gain Christ and to be found "in" Christ, presumably increasing his gain and his understanding of his place. Paul clearly states that he does not already have all that the good news offers (3:12). His ongoing purpose, he says, is to know Christ and the power of his resurrection and the fellowship of his sufferings.[39]

The point should not be missed, however, that Paul understands the loss of his past as a prelude to being "found in him" (3:9). Of equal importance is that we notice that Paul does not say that such loss is the same as sharing in Christ's sufferings; he rather says that this loss is what allows him to participate in them.

The stuff of Christ's sufferings, in which Paul longs to share, works with the stuff of Paul's new life "in" Christ, not of his past. The person who shares the sufferings of Christ is not the person he was. He is a person "in" Christ; the material on which afflictions now act is "in" Christ material. In fact, Paul describes himself after being found "in" Christ as one who no longer has his own righteousness based on the law, but the righteousness of God, which comes through the faith of Christ[40] and is based on faith (3:9). Paul, in other words, sees his "in" Christ self in radical distinction from what he was before. Now he is "in" Christ, before he was apart from Christ. Now he has a righteousness that is the very righteousness of God, before he had an inferior righteousness.[41]

38. So Fee, p. 320; κερδήσω and εὑρεθῶ, being in the aorist subjunctive in this purpose clause, convey the idea of future and of the present.

39. Cf. Bockmuehl, p. 208.

40. I here choose the subjective genitive rendering of πίστις Χριστοῦ (cf. also Bockmuehl, pp. 210-11). This reading adds a perspective while not taking anything away. The end of the verse clearly states the critical role of the believer's faith. It is further to be noted that my choice of the subjective genitive is not critical to the point of the present interpretation. Either way, Paul is saying that he is a new person as he participates in the sufferings of Christ.

41. K. Barth writes concerning 3:4-11: "Paul does not live as if he had found a new bridge from here to the beyond, from man to God, from destruction to redemption —

At the same time, Paul is aware that he is not yet perfect, that he must continue to hasten toward the prize of the upward call of God (3:14). Paul does not say that his growth in perfection requires his *suffering*. He says rather that his growth in perfection requires his *striving*. And he says that as one who strives he is one who has the righteousness of God and shares Christ's sufferings. It is as a person "in" Christ, righteous with God's righteousness, suffering with Christ's suffering, that he strives. This whole human package — the righteous sufferer — is who strives for the upward call of God. Paul says that his perfection will be achieved by this striving of one who has been seized by Christ (3:12). Subsequent to this seizure, suffering is part of his makeup. Suffering is *not* an instrument of sanctification, except insofar as it is part of the condition of the whole "in" Christ person. Paul directs his converts to strive in a similar way: "work out your own salvation with fear and quivering; for God is the one who energizes you both to will and to work for God's good purpose" (2:12-13).

Paul's Sufferings Resemble Christ's

Paul is certain that to have insight that his sufferings are "in Christ" (1:13) is at the same time to recognize that such sufferings resemble the sufferings of Christ. He supports his apology for his sufferings by saying that they resemble Christ's own. He furthermore suggests that the Philippians themselves know this both about his suffering and theirs.

In the course of the letter's first exhortation, Paul says that "it has been granted to you for the sake of Christ not only to believe in Christ but also to suffer representing Christ, having, in fact, the same struggle [as Christ], a struggle that you have seen and now hear to be mine" (1:29-30). As the immediately preceding demonstrates, the syntactical and grammatical territory of 1:29-30 is among the roughest in this letter. I

---

a new bridge alongside of which the old one could then very well be used again too on occasion. On the contrary, he lives in the knowledge that there is no bridge from here to *there*, but solely the way from there to *here*" (*Epistle to the Philippians*, tr. J. W. Leitch [Louisville: Westminster John Knox, 2002], p. 105).

make sense of it by reading "having the same struggle" as a reference to the struggle of suffering ὑπὲρ Χριστοῦ and by translating ὑπὲρ Χριστοῦ not as "for Christ's sake" (so NRSV) but as "representing Christ."[42] Paul's thought here is close to what he says later in 3:10 about participating in Christ's own suffering.[43] So here he does not give the *reason* for suffering[44] but explicates the meaning and significance of suffering as a believer. Paul claims that the Philippians already know that his own sufferings are validated by being in sync with those of the one at the center of the good news the Philippians themselves have embraced.

Paul's concern to make an apology for his sufferings by relating them to those of Christ is clear also from the manner in which he attacks the idea that circumcision can add value to faith in Christ. He does not argue against circumcision by citing Scripture or by appealing to the Philippians' experience of the Spirit or to their relationship with himself, as he does in Galatians. Rather, Paul describes the ludicrousness of those "in" Christ valuing or seeking security and comfort. Implied in his statement that he and like-minded others "do not trust in the flesh" (3:3) is his characterization of his opponents as people who are promising some sort of refuge from insecurities and troubles. Paul distinguishes himself and his converts from such folly by using himself as an example of one who achieved exemplary security in the flesh (3:4-6) and yet found that Christ offers something more valuable. The value Christ offers, as Paul himself proves, is anything but the capacity to trust in the flesh. The value Christ offers is (at least in part) the capacity to suffer.[45]

---

42. W. Bauer, *A Greek-English Lexicon of the New Testament and Other Early Christian Literature*, ed. F. W. Danker (Chicago: University of Chicago Press, 2000), p. 1030, notes that ὑπέρ with the genitive can mean "in place of, instead of, in the name of." My translation, then, reads the preposition as indicating representation.

43. Cf. Bockmuehl, p. 103.

44. Contra O'Brien, p. 159.

45. Occasionally we should remind ourselves in the midst of this study's focus on suffering that there is much more to the good news than the opportunity to share in Christ's suffering. As Paul says in Philippians, there is also encouragement, the incentive to love, participation in the Spirit, affection, and sympathy (2:1); Paul extols elsewhere other benefits, such as freedom from the power of sin and salvation in the day of the Lord.

It is not that Christ gives Paul and other believers an appetite for suffering. It is that Christ shares his sufferings (3:10). And Paul considers these sufferings to be much more valuable than anything he could secure in the flesh. The fellowship of Christ's sufferings is priceless, and Paul is sure that this treasure of partnership in Christ's sufferings outweighs by far what the opponents are offering. Security in the flesh — avoidance of suffering — is an ersatz investment that secures in the end nothing. On the other hand, when believers participate in Christ's own suffering, this will, as it did for Christ, lead to resurrection and life (3:11). What is plain to Paul, and what he wants to make plain to his converts, is that the gain Christ offers cannot be capitalized on without accepting the same loss as Christ did. Circumcision or any other action for or commitment to securing security in the flesh is woefully misguided. Paul is convinced that life and freedom from suffering will be achieved only by embracing the same afflictions as Christ — an embrace that clearly does not afford security in the flesh.

Paul's stated goal is not to avoid suffering but rather to know suffering. The suffering he wishes to know is the suffering of Christ. Paul defends the fittingness of his current weak and humiliated situation by extolling the necessity and value of partnership in Christ's suffering. It is only such partnership that will produce resurrection (3:10-11).

In the course of making an apology for his imprisonment by claiming that his sufferings are also Christ's, Paul bares before his Philippian converts the deepest desires of his life. He wishes that Christ be magnified in his body, whether in life or in death (1:20). Paul's conviction that his body is capable of exalting Christ reveals that Paul undergoes his current struggles in, with, and for Christ. Paul believes his body may endure afflictions in a manner that draws attention away from himself and instead shines a light on Christ. This is a remarkable idea, for the primary effect of bodily pain is to focus attention on that body, whether for the one whose body it is or for those who are witnessing the suffering. Paul's belief that his struggles will highlight not himself but Christ reveals how organically connected he knows himself to be to Christ.

This conviction of his essential rooting in Christ means for Paul that he partakes in the defining moments of Christ's drama. And so, while Paul desires nothing more than resurrection, he is convinced that it is not possible to have knowledge of the resurrection without knowledge also of Christ's sufferings: "that I may know him and the power of his resurrection and the fellowship of his sufferings" (3:10). Indeed, Paul considers it essential to become conformed to Christ's death.

Suffering in Conformity with Christ's Death

Paul's use of the participle συμμορφιζόμενος ("being conformed to, taking on the same form as") in connection with Christ's death (3:10) and in the same breath as speaking of his goal of knowing the power of Christ's resurrection and the fellowship of his sufferings, shows that conformity to Christ's death is the controlling factor in Paul's striving. The participle's present tense indicates an ongoing process: Paul regards the form of Christ's death as a continuing process that he experiences and that defines and shapes his knowledge of both Christ's resurrection and the partnership of Christ's sufferings. Thus, although Christ died at a particular instant, the form of Christ's death will be experienced not in an instant, but through the course of a life.

Furthermore, the fact that the participle is anarthrous indicates that Paul is describing the *circumstances* in which knowledge of Christ's resurrection and of the fellowship of his sufferings may take place. It is in the process of taking on the form of Christ's death that Paul can be on target for his goal of knowing both Christ's resurrection and partnership in Christ's suffering.

The form of Christ's death is shaped not by the pain of others but the power of life. Being governed by the form of Christ's death, the essential feature of Christ-like suffering is its effect. Readers of Paul in Philippians typically regard the central feature of Christ-like suffering to be its cause: it is suffering that comes from being focused on others.[46] As we

46. According to Fee, for instance, Paul thinks that his sufferings reflect Christ's in so far as they, like Christ's, are focused on others: Christ's sufferings were for our sake

have seen, Paul's words in 1 Thessalonians support this view. However, nowhere in Philippians does Paul say that Christ suffered or died for our sake.[47] Paul's description of Christ's suffering in Philippians is of a kind of suffering that has an astonishing result: vindication for Christ (2:9-11),[48] glory for God (2:11), and resurrection from the dead for himself and others (3:10-11). As described in Philippians, the shape of Christ's suffering and death is determined not by their cause but by what they lead to: resurrection, vindication, and God's glory.[49] It must be, then, that those who share in Christ's suffering, being conformed to Christ's death, will also suffer in expectation of vindication, life, and glorifying God.

The circumstances that require Paul to make an apology for his sufferings as actually confirming the good news (1:7b)[50] also require that he keep the glow of the resurrection in view. Paul has come to see that suffering in partnership with Christ is suffering that is qualitatively different from suffering apart from Christ. He emphasizes not that he, like Christ, suffers for others. He underscores rather that sharing the sufferings of Christ, being conformed to the death of Christ, is shaped not by the pain of others but by the power of life. The result of Christ's death

---

and Paul's are for the sake of the gospel (pp. 332-33, n. 64; cf. Hawthorne, p. 148). F. F. Bruce goes so far as to suggest that it was Paul's hope to absorb as many of the sufferings of Christ as he could so that he might "leave less for his fellow Christians to endure" (p. 91).

47. O'Brien also notices that 3:10 does not refer to Christ's redemptive death (p. 405). The absence of sacrificial language is among the reasons to be cautious about E. Lohmeyer's proposal that this hymn was originally sung at the eucharist *(Kyrios Jesus)*.

48. Cf. Bloomquist, p. 196.

49. It may be that the positive effects of Christ's suffering and death as Paul outlines them in Philippians are another way of saying what he says elsewhere about, for instance, Christ's death defeating sin's power (e.g., Rom 3:23-25). The point to be noticed, however, is that Paul avoids referring in this letter to the sacrificial or vicarious aspect of Christ's death and focuses instead on the vindication and life that result from them.

50. Reading this part of the verse as "while in my chains, even (i.e., which are) in the defense and confirmation of the gospel." This reading is confirmed by Paul's reference to his imprisonment as an ἀπολογία (1:16).

is Christ's life and publicly acknowledged divinity.[51] Moreover, Christ's death ends in giving glory to God (2:11).

In relating his sufferings to those of Christ (1:29) and stating that he desires to share in Christ's sufferings (3:10), Paul interprets the pain of his fetters as capable of transforming death into life, of revealing Christ's identity (cf. 1:20), and ultimately of glorifying God. Paul, like Christ, suffers so that life may come and so that God may be glorified.

The form of Christ's death is the form of God's death. The form of Christ's death is not the manner of that death.[52] It is to be noticed that Paul does not here speak of *co-crucifixion* (cf. Gal 2:20). Instead, Paul's reference to the form of Christ's death calls to mind not *how* Christ died but what that death revealed and achieved. Paul emphasizes that Christ's death is a death in the context of life; he surrounds reference to Christ's death with references to resurrection, thereby underscoring that the form of Christ's death transformed his death into life (2:10-11). Paul's song about the form in which Christ accepted death — he was in the form of God but he took the form of a servant; he did not regard

---

51. Paul writes that God bestowed on Christ "the name that is above every name" and that in the future every knee will bow at that name (2:9-10). Christ's God-bestowed name is a divine name (cf. Bockmuehl, p. 142), which does not, as Silva notes, compromise Israel's monotheistic faith, for the name Jesus bears is the name of the one Lord and he bears it for the glory of God the Father (p. 131; cf. Martin, p. 283). See also L. Hurtado, who notes that this passage's "creative use of Is. 45.23 . . . as predicting a universal acknowledgement of Jesus as *Kyrios* shows that being given this title must be the Greek equivalent to bearing the OT name of God" (*Lord Jesus Christ: Devotion to Jesus in Earliest Christianity* [Grand Rapids: Eerdmans, 2003], p. 112).

52. Contra Cassidy, p. 187. Cassidy claims that Paul's reference to the form of Christ's death indicates Paul's insight that "his life and ministry might end almost exactly in the manner in which Jesus' own earthly life had ended" (p. 187), that Paul has come to see that "Jesus' death by capital sentence at the hands of the Roman authorities" will be his fate also (pp. 187-88). This suggestion helpfully stresses the radical and concrete way in which Paul understood fellowship with Christ's sufferings, but its effect is to equate the "form of Christ's death" with Roman execution. Where Paul refers explicitly to the manner in which Christ died (Gal 2:20) it is clear that he applies crucifixion to himself only analogically: he has been crucified together with Christ; this death has already taken place and is a continuing influence in his (continuing) life.

being equal to God as something to take advantage of[53] but humbly and obediently went to death on a cross — extols the form of Christ's death as the form of God's death.[54] It is as one equal to God that Christ dies. As K. Barth writes concerning this verse, the "equality of Christ with God is . . . the fixed, *ultimate* background from which his road sets out and to which it returns."[55]

What Christ's death reveals is how God suffers and dies;[56] what Christ's death achieved is life and the capacity for all to see God's glory. The form of Christ's death, then, is anything but morbid, defeatist, or even sad. The form of Christ's death is, paradoxically, the form of life. It is God who is revealed in Christ's death.

Paul himself suffers in conformity with Christ's death. Paul's desire to be conformed to this death is embodied in his wish (1:19) and hope (2:23-24) to be delivered from prison. This hopeful and positive response to his imprisonment is a concrete example of sharing the sufferings of Christ while being conformed to the shape of Christ's death. Paul suffers not in despair, but in hope that there is deliverance from suffering. Furthermore, his repeated references to his joy[57] and encouragements to the Philippians to be joyful[58] reveal that Paul's suffering was shaped not by suffering itself but by his faith that life comes through such suffering. Paul's suffering is laced with joy be-

---

53. Following N. T. Wright, ἁρπαγμός means not grasping or clinging but taking advantage *based* on equality with God. Wright translates this portion of the hymn: "Christ did not consider his equality with God as something to take advantage of" ("Jesus Christ Is Lord: Philippians 2.5-11," in *The Climax of the Covenant: Christ and the Law in Pauline Theology* [Minneapolis: Fortress, 1992], pp. 56-98, here p. 79).

54. I am aware that this statement wades into the longstanding theopaschite controversy. See on this J. Pelikan, *The Christian Tradition: A History of the Development of Doctrine* (Chicago: University of Chicago Press, 1971), I, pp. 270-71.

55. *Philippians*, p. 61.

56. While not referring to this text, but to Phil 1:23, Ignatius reads something similar in Paul's words: "allow me to be an imitator of the suffering of my God" (*Romans* 6:3, translation from W. R. Schoedel, *Ignatius of Antioch* [Hermeneia; Philadelphia: Fortress, 1985], p. 181).

57. 1:4, 18; 2:2, 17; 4:1, 10.

58. 1:25; 2:17, 18, 28, 29; 3:1; 4:4.

cause it is suffering circumscribed by the form of Christ's victorious death.

In his apology for his imprisonment Paul is in essence asking his converts to interpret his current circumstances as the process of taking on the form of Christ's death. Paul's ongoing afflictions are in partnership with Christ and are shaped by the form of Christ's death, which, though gruesome — "even death on a cross" (2:8) — was the death God would have.

Believers Suffer Together

Paul's defense of his humiliating and painful chains evolves beyond the claim that they are experienced "in Christ," beyond the claim that they are a participation in Christ's suffering, to the insight that his suffering is shared with that of other believers. Mulling over his choice[59] whether to go on living in the flesh or to die, Paul admits that, while death is gain (1:21) and he does desire to depart and be with Christ (1:23), nevertheless he sees that his responsibility is to remain in the flesh on account of the Philippians (1:24). His acceptance of his responsibility to remain in the flesh on behalf of his converts is at the same time an acceptance of his responsibility to suffer with them, for, as Paul makes plain throughout this letter, being "in" Christ *and* in this life (in the flesh) is to suffer.

Paul sees his suffering as capable of mingling with the afflictions the Philippians themselves know.[60] He expresses his willingness to be poured out as a libation on the sacrifice and service of the Philippians' faith (2:17), that is, on their suffering.[61] The Philippians' faith involves their suffering (1:28-30), and Paul is willing to participate in it. Like a

---

59. Note Paul's use of the verb αἱρέω, 1:22.

60. Cf. Bockmuel, p. 161, who reads Paul here to be saying that his struggles "complement" those of the Philippians.

61. Fee also interprets the reference to sacrifice in 2:17 as indicating that the Philippians are suffering (p. 255). There are reasons to be cautious about understanding Paul's meaning here to be that he is anxious for martyrdom; see again Fee, pp. 252-54.

drink offering poured on a sacrifice, so Paul offers to add his suffering to the Philippians' own.[62]

It is to be noted that Paul does not say that the reason he suffers is to take away or relieve the troubles of the Philippians. He says rather that he will add (2:17) or continue (1:25) his suffering on account of them. Paul suffers "in Christ" (1:13), and while this entails suffering along with others "in" Christ, Paul does not say that this suffering is caused by others' pain or that it can take away others' pain. Likewise, Paul's encouragement that the Philippians pray for his release from prison (1:19) is an invitation for *them* to participate in *his* present suffering.[63]

Moreover, Paul encourages his converts to see that they, like he, share in the afflictions of others who are "in" Christ.[64] Paul interprets the Philippians' attention to his needs in prison as a sharing in his affliction (4:14) and their aid to him through Epaphroditus as a sacrifice (4:18). Implied in Paul's use here of the word "sacrifice" is that what the Philippians gave him came in the midst of their suffering. Earlier Paul speaks of the Philippians' sacrifice and service for the faith (2:17). Thus, though they themselves were suffering, they reached out to Paul in his troubles. In the course of caring for Paul, Epaphroditus suffered to the point of death, causing the Philippians concern (2:26, 27, 30). Paul here affirms that the Philippians have enacted, and are continuing to exhibit, the intention he himself expresses of mingling with other believers' sufferings (2:17). His commendation of the reciprocity the Philippians demonstrate (4:15-17) and his conviction that their prayers will help accomplish his deliverance from jail (1:19) contribute to this affirmation.

---

62. While the libation in Greco-Roman cults and Judaism was often poured on at the end of the sacrificial sequence, it is unclear what that might signify here. It is saying too much, as Hawthorne does, that the libation completed the sacrifice. This over-interpretation leads to Hawthorne's over-reading of 2:17 as Paul saying his sufferings act "as a seal" on the Philippians' sacrificial service (p. 106). See, on the other hand, T. W. Manson's rendering of Paul's meaning: "we are all . . . in the same straits" ("St. Paul in Ephesus: The Date of the Epistle to the Philippians," *Bulletin of the John Rylands Library* 23 [1939]: 182-200, here p. 185).

63. It is to be noted that Paul's manner of request for their prayers exhibits his conviction that, as his suffering is "in Christ," it *has deliverance* in view.

64. Cf. Fowl, "Believing Forms Seeing," p. 329.

Paul encourages the Philippians to recognize that their life is now (rightly) shaped by the mutuality of suffering, for they, like he, are sharing the afflictions of Christ.

Paul Exhorts the Philippians to Engage in the Same Struggle He Knows

Paul's apology for his suffering is both a defense and an exhortation. He needs to clear the air with his converts so that they can see the appropriateness of his circumstances in light of Christ, and he also is concerned to encourage them to engage in the same struggle he knows. What he wishes to hear about them is that, like athletes, they are striving together for the gospel in the face of enemies, that they are living according to their true identity (πολιτεύεσθε) and so bravely facing their opponents (1:27-28). He encourages them to see that the suffering that comes with such courage is a gift, a gift that allows them to represent Christ (1:29-30). They, like Paul, are privileged to share the sufferings of Christ.

Paul goes beyond exhorting the Philippians to regard their sufferings as a fitting privilege: he commands that they take on suffering. He directs his converts to have the same disposition (φρονεῖτε) as Christ,[65] a disposition allowing one to empty oneself willingly, become a servant, humble oneself, and die a torturous death (2:5-8).[66]

---

65. φρονέω is the verb related to the noun φρόνησις. This word and its concept, of course, plays a prominent role in Greco-Roman moral philosophy. Its basic meaning is "practical reasoning." I use the word "disposition" to indicate what I take to be the understood aim of practical reasoning in Paul's time: to create inner motivations that choose the most fitting actions.

66. Cf. W. A. Meeks: "this letter's most comprehensive purpose is the shaping of a Christian *phronesis*, a practical moral reasoning that is 'conformed to [Christ's] death' in hope of his resurrection" ("The Man from Heaven in Paul's Letter to the Philippians," in *The Future of Early Christianity: Essays in Honor of Helmut Koester*, ed. B. A. Pearson [Minneapolis: Fortress, 1991], pp. 329-36, here p. 333).

The Communion of Suffering and Joy

Paul's sense of the organic nature of believers' suffering means that his defense and explanation of his own sufferings involves speaking of them as inextricably connected to the sufferings of Christ and the sufferings of others who are "in" Christ. The struggle believers know is a joint one — the Philippians share the same ἀγών as Paul (and Christ, 1:30). The suffering of one "in" Christ mingles with the suffering of the many "in" Christ. Paul does not conceive of solitary suffering "in" Christ.

The connectedness Paul affirms among believers extends beyond their suffering to their response to their suffering. For Paul, joy is the fitting response to suffering "in" Christ, and he considers this joy not an individual experience but a shared one (2:17-18). The mutual reaction of joy to sharing in the sufferings of Christ is due to the nature of these sufferings.

While, as Paul himself exemplifies, it is as individuals that people are seized by Christ (3:12), the "ego" that subsequently speaks, acts, experiences, and believes is rooted in a being other than himself or herself. And so Paul can say that he is self-sufficient in the same breath as saying that he is empowered by Christ (4:11-13). (Noting this fact alone is enough to call into question the idea that Paul has a Stoical attitude to suffering.)[67] And, since the distinguishing feature of believers' suffering is that it terminates in life and vindication and God's glory, the communal response will be joy. Such suffering is suffering in companionship, and the joyful response to it will be collective.

The intensity of Paul's apology reveals the difficulty of understanding or enacting the reality of our communion in both suffering and joy. Moreover, Paul's appeal to love as the vehicle that allows others to see the reality of his own situation (1:16) is both a recognition that, looked at coldly, his afflictions challenge the gospel's power and that it takes the connection accomplished by love to see things aright. It is love that gives knowledge and insight (1:9), allowing recognition both of the

67. Cf. O'Brien, p. 527.

source of other believers' sufferings and of how they may be an apology for the gospel. Love's capacity to create communion is essential for understanding and experiencing gospel suffering.

Suffering of Nonbelievers

Paul expresses next to no concern in this letter for those apart from Christ. The circumstances of and purposes for his writing seem to concentrate his mind almost exclusively on suffering as a believer and as a result of being a believer. What little there is on the topic of the suffering of humanity apart from Christ is somewhat confusing. At two points Paul speaks about people he deems to be outside Christ, and in both instances he predicts their destruction (1:28 and 3:19). While not addressing their current suffering this indicates that Paul's conception of the good news includes *future* suffering for those who oppose it. At the same time, Paul says that Christ's vindication after suffering and death means "that every tongue may confess that Jesus Christ is Lord" (2:11). These words at face value say that no person will be excluded from the salvation that attends confession of Christ as Lord. Whether or not this is what Paul meant[68] and, if he did, whether the confession of all will be voluntary is a matter of debate. Likewise, whether or not Paul meant that every tongue *should* confess or *will* confess is also a question mark.[69] Furthermore, the relation of this statement to others of Paul, such as 1 Cor 15:24-28, where he claims that everything will be subjected to Christ, could keep the scholarly mind fruitfully engaged for some time.

These few hints in Philippians about what Paul thinks of the suffering of nonbelievers may, however, allow us to hear at least a whisper of his thought. We might first notice that when Paul does talk about future suffering for those who oppose the good news he does not judge that

68. Fee says there is "no hint that those who bow are acknowledging his salvation" (p. 224).

69. There are two possibilities: that "confess" is in the aorist subjunctive or the variant reading where the verb appears in the future indicative.

these opponents are already damned. He rather warns of the possibility of such. While Paul regards destruction as the end of those who live as enemies of the cross of Christ (3:18), he holds out the possibility that those who have rejected the gospel might become aware of the stakes in doing so. Confronted with people living the faith of the gospel, these "enemies" may have a *sign* of the nature of their circumstances (1:27-28). (It is to be noted that the sign [ἔνδειξις] is for *their* advantage: αὐτοῖς.) In other words, Paul is not so much declaring whom God does and does not save as he is clarifying that it is through the gospel that God saves.

What may be said at the very least is that Paul is convinced that God will finally resolve things so that all acknowledge, in one way or another, that it is Jesus Christ who is Lord and that this will result in the glory of God. This resolution is to the benefit of all — Jesus Christ, God, and humanity in general. Paul's conviction focuses his attention on salvation rather than damnation. Paul's sights are on God's completion of deliverance, when suffering is finally abolished. He appears to hope that this liberation will be known by all.

The fact that nonbelievers currently know suffering is not mentioned by Paul. And he gives no indication that he thinks his present suffering is in any way alleviating the current suffering of humanity. However, it may be that Paul did hope that by its being in conformity with Christ's death, his present suffering could be part of ensuring that life in all its fullness will be known by humanity in general.

The fact is that in Philippians Paul is not much interested in any suffering other than his own (with the occasional nod to that of the congregation at Philippi). This suggests, as noted before, that the fact of Paul's suffering was problematic for the Philippians. It may also have been a problem for Paul. That he provides such a conceptually expansive interpretation of his own suffering implies that Paul needed not only to make a defense for the sake of his converts but also for himself; at some point Paul had reached an impasse that required that he explain to himself the strange situation of a person "in" Christ experiencing afflictions.[70]

---

70. Cf. R. T. Fortna, "Philippians: Paul's Most Egocentric Letter," in *The Conversation Continues* (n. 6 above), pp. 220-34, here p. 221.

Summary

On the basis of Philippians, what little that can be said about Paul's view of the suffering of nonbelievers suggests that he did not relish it, but neither did he reflect much on it. In Philippians Paul's gaze is fixed chiefly on his own suffering, although it does extend at times to the suffering of his converts.

The limits of Paul's horizon serve to enhance the shades and contours of that to which he does turn his eyes. We see Paul placing the miserable and shameful situation of his imprisonment in the radiant light of the resurrection. He does not lay blame anywhere or on anyone for his predicament. He certainly does not describe his situation with the language of persecution, that is, victimization. He says rather that his chains are "in Christ" (1:13) and that he wishes for sufferings that resemble Christ's own (3:10). Moreover, as Christ's sufferings and death resulted in vindication, resurrection, and God's glory, Paul embraces his sufferings in like manner. It is with joy that he suffers, not because he enjoys the process of suffering — he hopes for deliverance from prison — but because he knows that Christ-like suffering will produce the end of suffering and death. He suffers not for suffering's sake but for life's sake.

His suffering, in fact, resembles the suffering that God would undertake, for in resembling Christ's suffering, Paul suffers in companionship with the one who suffered as equal to God. Paul's suffering is, then, qualitatively different from the suffering of one apart from Christ. In fact, the suffering he seeks to explain to himself and others begins only after he has lost what defined him before Christ grasped him for his own. The suffering he as one "found in [Christ]" (3:9) knows is suffering that works on and in a new person. It is not suffering that works to sanctify the old person. It is suffering that works with a person who has God's own righteousness so that he may know resurrection from the dead.

It must be emphasized that Paul's meditation in Philippians does not present the suffering necessary for resurrection life as serving the purpose of purifying or purging the past from the believer. Paul thinks that his past is already gone by the time he is found in Christ.

Paul sees his suffering as shaped by the form of Christ's death —
that death which ended in vindication and resurrection and God's glory.
It is, then, not just that such suffering is suffering *for the sake of* life; it is
that this suffering is *shaped by, circumscribed by,* life. The resurrection is
both the shaper and the outcome of believers' suffering. And it is as the
person "in" Christ suffers within the contours defined by the resurrection that that person is made fit to "attain the resurrection from the
dead" (3:11).

This makes joy the fitting response to believers' suffering. For such
suffering is sure that suffering will end in the glorious expanse of God's
life. Believers know that the resurrection comes only because of
Christ's suffering, and so it is a grace to be able to share these sufferings.
The resurrection is possible only after Christ's death, and believers in
Christ are gifted with being able to be conformed to that death. Joy is
exactly the right response to this gift.

Believers together know both Christ's afflictions and their joyful response to this gift. Believers may also know that their suffering is never
solitary: their individual sharing in the sufferings of Christ is also suffering along with others who are suffering "in" Christ. Believers do not,
nor can they, take away each other's pain, but they may share it. Love's
role is critical here, for it is loving fellow believers that provides insight
into the transformative reality of their pain.

Using Philippians to Talk about Suffering

Vast and deep is the Christian tradition of using Philippians to talk
about suffering. The text of Philippians has been understood as promoting martyrdom, either real[71] or martyrdom of a bloodless variety[72]

71. Ignatius of Antioch, for instance, refers to Phil 2:17 in his plea not to be saved
from martyrdom: "Grant me nothing more than to be poured out as a libation for God
while an altar is still ready" (*Romans* 2:2).

72. Bloomquist, p. 25, cites G. M. Colombas's reflection on the changing circumstances of Christians for whom the ideal of physical martyrdom became next to impossible after Constantine: "Since the grace of the martyr is not given to all and persecu-

that arises from sacrificial service to others[73] or is self-induced.[74] Paul's words to the Philippians have been heard as an encouragement to Christian witness at the cost of suffering.[75] Philippians has also been used to nurture hope that through suffering the believer will be perfected.[76] This letter has also served to explain or encourage the continuing struggle of the believer.[77] Paul's letter reveals its potency by the fact it has been capable of provoking many and varied impassioned meditations on the suffering of Christians.

Assurance in Suffering

My reading would point to a use of this letter that first reckons with the cruciform shape of the Christian life. The good news announces the future defeat of suffering and death in the midst of the present continuance of suffering and death. The cross remains at the heart of the gospel; suffering is a given for believers. Acknowledging this is not a call to

---

tions become scarcer, the idea that Christian life lived in generosity and self-denial is itself a confession of faith — a bloodless martyrdom — begins to take root" (*El monacato primitive* [Madrid: Biblioteca de autores cristianos, 1974], I, p. 31).

73. Fee comments on Phil 3:8 that "those who follow Christ will . . . likewise have to 'bear the cross' on behalf of others" (p. 333).

74. For instance, the promotion of mortification of the flesh: the medieval Bishop Haymo of Halberstadt paraphrases Phil 1:20: "If I sustain torments, all those who hear will say: Great is this God, for whose name his servants are not afraid to die" (cited in Bloomquist, p. 26).

75. Tertullian encourages Christian witness even at the cost of martyrdom, referring to Paul's words to the Philippians (*Scorpiace* 13, in *Ante-Nicene Fathers* [Grand Rapids: Eerdmans, reprint], III, p. 647).

76. Irenaeus refers to Phil 3:10 in his exhortation to deny self and so be "borne onward to perfection" (*Fragment 31*, in *Ante-Nicene Fathers*, I, p. 574). Augustine alludes to Phil 2:8 in his call for humility as the key to reaching "the Word by whom all things were made" (*Sermon 67.17*, in *Nicene and Post-Nicene Fathers*, VI, p. 464). J. B. Lightfoot, reading Phil 1:19, comments that Paul's trials "will develop the spiritual life in the Apostle, will be a pathway to the glories of heaven" (p. 91).

77. Polycarp alludes to Phil 2:16 in his exhortation to patience in suffering (*Philippians 9*).

search out suffering. Neither should this recognition be used to validate increasing suffering for oneself or others. Nor should this understanding be used to excuse compromise or apathy in regard to justice. Rather, the recognition that being a Christian does not separate one from suffering functions chiefly to comfort Christian sufferers. Our suffering is not a sign of our failure. Philippians encourages us to look our suffering in the face and reckon with it as part of the shape of our life "in" Christ.

The chief use of this letter is, then, one of assurance. *The Christian sufferer is not out of step with the gospel.*

I have emphasized repeatedly my understanding that Paul understood his suffering to be "in" Christ. I understand this to be the case for Paul because he knows *himself* to be "in" Christ. He finds himself and wants to find himself "in" Christ: "I have suffered the loss of all things, and count them as refuse, in order that I may gain Christ and be found *in him*" (3:8-9). There is no easy way to reword Paul's words without over-interpretation, over-simplification, or emphasizing nuances that may not be there. Calvin is wise on this point: referring to 1 Cor 1:9, where Paul gives thanks for the Corinthians' having been "called into the fellowship of [God's] Son," Calvin writes: "how it happens, I confess is far above the measure of my intelligence. Hence I adore the mystery rather than labor to understand it."[78]

What is clear is that Paul views everything in his life, including his suffering, as part of his new reality "in" Christ. As a consequence, Paul radically redefines the ostensible power dynamics of his situation; while the civic authorities may have put him in chains, Paul knows and experiences his fetters not as their doing but "in" Christ. He does not seek to dignify or defend his circumstances by blaming them on other people's anger toward the gospel. Paul rather accepts his suffering as part and parcel of being "in" Christ.

Moreover, Paul does not single out his situation of suffering as having more status than the Philippians'. He and the Philippians share the

---

78. Calvin to Peter Martyr, August 8, 1555, quoted from B. Gerrish, *Grace and Gratitude: The Eucharistic Theology of John Calvin* (Minneapolis: Fortress, 1993), p. 128.

same struggle (1:30). Paul's current imprisonment and the Philippians' struggle, whatever it is, are particular manifestations of the cross at the heart of the gospel.

Implicit in Paul's response to his suffering in Philippians is the conviction that the horizon of reality is broader than what can be seen in the suffering moment. The horizon of God's reality is framed by life. Paul is convinced that if we suffer "in" Christ, sharing Christ's sufferings, even then we will come to see and be embraced by this reality. Such suffering is limited by the certainty of deliverance from suffering. And, moreover, Paul is certain that the end of suffering is not just a silent black screen on which appear the words "the End." The end of suffering is rather a gloriously radiant life. This conviction does not require that we pretend that our suffering is not bitter. In fact, as mentioned, a Stoical approach is quite at odds with my reading of Philippians. The acceptance of suffering does indeed recognize pain and loss.

Consequently, this letter addresses believers' afflictions of whatever sort (imprisonment, loss, illness, and so forth, most of which in the North Atlantic context appear to have nothing directly to do with being a Christian). Philippians addresses the reality that belief in the gospel does not insulate us from various kinds of troubles.

Before continuing, it is important to identify some ways in which Philippians should not be used. First, Philippians does not provide comfort for the wrongdoer. It does not speak to the suffering that comes from wrongdoing. This letter's assurance is for the bewildered Christian sufferer — the one who asks in the face of suffering, why me, why this? The drunk driver who kills a child, the spouse who rages against or beats his or her partner, and so on will not find in Philippians consolation regarding their subsequent suffering. Paul does not here address the issue of the guilty sufferer.

Second, Philippians is not a warrant for being a victim or a victimizer. Paul's encouragement to face our suffering is not an endorsement of abuse or of accepting abuse. Paul does not see himself as a victim, and his words may not be used to sanction either victimization or victimhood.

Philippians Offers Atypical Explanations for the Suffering of Believers

Paul's words may challenge more familiar explanations for Christian suffering. Among the more typical are: in some way we are responsible for our own suffering, and, closely related to this, our suffering is a punishment; or suffering is good for us, for it makes us better people; or Satan is the cause of Christian suffering; or, nonbelievers are the cause of Christian suffering; or Christians must suffer like Christ suffers, for others and in order to help heal the world.[79] As I have read Paul in Philippians, he does not address suffering as a believer or as a result of being a believer in any of these ways.

Suffering Is Neither Punishment Nor Purge

Paul exhibits no sense of guilt or responsibility for his current predicament. Philippians may, then, be used to allay Christian sufferers' fear that their suffering is the result of their having done something wrong[80] or having not believed well or hard enough. As Paul speaks here, suffering is not a punishment for past sins, nor is it an antidote to a believer's current soul sickness. Paul speaks as one who has the righteousness of God (3:9). It is as a person already seized by Christ and now found in him that Paul strains toward his prize of the upward call of God. Suffering's purpose is not to purge his sin-sick soul or to punish it. As mentioned more than once, for Paul his suffering is shaped by the form of Christ's death. Such suffering serves the purpose neither of purifying nor of punishing the individual. Its purpose is rather to produce life.

The distinction may be hard to grasp. Paul's statement that the purpose of sharing in Christ's sufferings is so that he can achieve the resur-

---

79. See J. C. Beker for various biblical views on suffering (*Suffering and Hope: The Biblical Vision and the Human Predicament* [Grand Rapids: Eerdmans, 1987]).

80. Again, Paul's words do not address the situation of one who *does* suffer for doing wrong.

rection has sometimes been read to mean that such sufferings get him ready for resurrection by cleansing him of sin.[81] However, we have noticed that not only does Paul *not* make the connection between sharing in Christ's sufferings and dealing with his own sin but also that what Paul *does* say is that it is as one who has the righteousness of God that he shares in Christ's sufferings. Philippians may then be used to discredit the idea that there is a virtue to suffering in and of itself, for it is either legitimate punishment for past wrongs, or it makes us into better people.

Paul embraces suffering not for suffering's sake but for Christ's sake. And he expects that this embrace will produce life. His response to the sting of suffering is completely non-self-focused. His suffering does not make him introspective, but Christ-focused. He sees his suffering not as the result of his failings but as part of his life "in" Christ. This strange response liberates him, as it may liberate other Christian sufferers, from drawing inward in response to suffering. It may free us from getting drawn into the vortex of suffering, seeing ourselves as the center around which pain and loss swirl. Our suffering is not our fault, and so we need not focus on ourselves, but on the one in whom we live, the one who will bring life out of the darkest and most painful experiences.

For the believer, the experience of suffering, whatever its cause, may focus on making us fit for resurrection life. This fitness requires *not the purging of sin and wickedness from our souls and bodies, but our being shaped into beings dominated by life and not by death.* Perhaps this is saying the same thing from two different perspectives, but the point of perspective Paul chooses is what is here instructive. In Philippians, Paul draws attention to Christ's death — a death that Paul describes not as for sins but for life.[82] The suffering we will know as believers may, if we recognize the fact and allow ourselves to undergo the process, change us into people who radiate light and life because we actually are out of

81. E.g., Hawthorne, pp. 147-48.

82. Elsewhere Paul does draw connections between sin and death and between life and freedom from sin. Those texts have a different use for the Christian believer. My point is that Philippians' usefulness is for circumstances where comfort and hope are the most fitting response to the Christian sufferer.

the shadow of death. Paul does not dissect this mystery but only states it. Suffering, he is convinced, is circumscribed by life. Life, and not suffering, may be the controlling factor of the experience of suffering. The desire for life and deliverance and the conviction that life and deliverance are imminent draw suffering into a circle of light from which it would otherwise be excluded. Such an understanding challenges believers to hope and to find the life that is present even in the midst of pain.

Believers Do Not Suffer Because They Are Targets of Others or of the Devil

Paul not only does not blame himself for his suffering, he blames neither Satan nor other people. This observation may help redirect Christians' gaze away from their enemies, their competitors, their betrayers, or even the devil. In fact, the discovery that Paul does not lay blame for his suffering anywhere at all is pedagogically and pastorally important. Paul's words in Philippians encourage Christian sufferers not to feel victimized. It is to be noticed that such an acceptance of suffering in Paul's case, rather than flattening out emotions or deadening hopes, does rather the opposite. As Paul's striking use of images from the world of the athlete show, acceptance of suffering goes hand-in-hand with the thrill of pursuit of the goal,[83] striving toward God's radiant life.

As I read Paul's words there is not an ounce of defeatism or Stoicism. He longs for life in the midst of his pain; he longs for deliverance from prison; he believes suffering will end. He accepts suffering while striving with every ounce of his energy. He accepts suffering not because that is the wisest way to respond to the nature of things as they are. Rather he accepts suffering because it is through sharing Christ's suffering that the end of suffering will be accomplished. Paul suffers forward, toward a goal. His acceptance of suffering is not acquiescence. His acceptance of suffering is a sign of hope and an act of faith.

---

83. Barth aptly comments: "If there is one man who know *no* passivity, then it is the *symmorphizomenos to thanato Christou* (the man who enters into the form of Christ's death)" (p. 106).

Believers Are Not Required to Suffer for the Salvation of Others

Given that Philippians does not relate Christ-like suffering to suffering that saves others, explaining Christian suffering as necessary for the sake of saving others misses the mark of Paul's words here. The importance of staying on the mark is that this can spare Christians from expending energy in wrong directions. Paul's words here, thankfully, do not endorse messiah complexes, the sense of needing to suffer to save others from pain. Christian suffering is in concert with other Christians, but, as Paul describes it in Philippians, it cannot take away other believers' pain. Christians share the afflictions of other Christians, but sharing the pain is very different from taking it on with the goal of taking it away. The former respects that each believer has his or her own journey toward God (albeit a journey shared with other believers) — a journey that will involve suffering. The latter tries to walk a believer's path for that person. In the latter there is a certain disrespect for the suffering believer, a lack of trust in God, and a rather hubristic heroism. The further danger of the view that Christians are required to take away or take on the pain of others is its potential to be used as an endorsement for believers to accept abuse. Acceptance of suffering as a believer is a completely different thing from suffering as a result of acquiescence to unjust or abusive treatment.[84]

Is Christ to Blame?

It is worth asking whether Paul's conviction that his suffering is "in" Christ leads Christian sufferers to blame Christ for their troubles. Paul does not take his thoughts there. Rather, he sees Christ's sufferings as the necessary prelude to Christ's vindication, resurrection for those who believe in him, and the capacity of all to glorify God. Paul is silent before

84. As mentioned above, acceptance of suffering "in" Christ is *not* also acceptance of injustice for oneself or others.

the mystery of why God should have organized reality in such a way that Christ's suffering was required. Paul speaks instead about the wondrous results of such suffering. Not an ounce of anger can be detected in Paul's reflections on suffering. This is not to say, of course, that Paul never expresses anger against opponents who are thwarting or abusing him or his gospel. It is rather to comment on the remarkable fact that, though Paul reckons that he has taken on suffering by being taken in hand by Christ, he does not complain but rather rejoices. His response to his own suffering is one option for how we too may respond.

Conclusion

Paul's words in Philippians may be used to help Christians reshape the understanding and experience of their particular sufferings. Whether they be the tragedies of death, the humiliations of age, the challenges of illness or poverty, believers may suffer knowing that the power of life is greater than the power of suffering and death. This may affect the present experience of affliction, allowing the affliction to produce life both in the person who suffers and those to whom he or she is connected. *One of the manifestations of this life will be the seeking and hoping for deliverance from suffering.*

Suffering may shape one into a person fit for resurrection. When believers suffer they are becoming people who may know the power of God's never-ending life. This suffering is not a choice but part of the package of being "in" Christ. What *is* a matter of choice is whether or not to recognize and embrace and participate in this suffering. Presumably, the fact that Paul needed to exhort the Philippian believers to embrace his understanding of suffering indicates that it is entirely possible for Christians to suffer blindly, unaware of the wondrous potential and gift of sharing in the same struggle as Christ's.

Paul's identification of the critical role love plays in understanding his suffering further indicates how easy it is to misunderstand the source and significance of suffering. The paradox of joyful response to suffering is solved once love opens our eyes to who we are suffering in, who we are suffering with, and what we are suffering for. We suffer not in lonely isolation but "in" Christ, with Christ, and with other believers. We suffer for life. We suffer forward, for the life of God, whose glory we will see in the day when suffering's term is ended.

Paul in chains stands before the mystery that God is not absent when Paul suffers.

4

ROMANS

We Too Groan

———

Romans does not portray nearly so neat a divide between the suffering of believers and of nonbelievers as I have suggested we might see in 1 Thessalonians and Philippians. In this letter, one of his last, written after years of experience of living the life of faith in Christ and of witnessing others attempt the same, Paul has come to see that believers and nonbelievers share in common both a history of suffering and a present experience of suffering.[1] While for Paul there is, subsequent to Christ's death and resurrection, a new and distinctive manner and mode of human suffering, for him this does not mean that the suffering of those who believe in that death and resurrection shares nothing in common with the suffering of unbelievers. In fact, quite to the contrary, Paul's mature consideration is that there is something of an identification of believers and nonbelievers precisely in their suffering.

We will, therefore, begin this chapter by summarizing the common tribulations all humanity knows, as portrayed by Paul in Romans. After

1. My thematic study means that some of the major themes that concern Paul in Romans and have been the focus of endless scholarly studies — themes such as the law, the righteousness of God, righteousness by faith, Israel, etc. — are not addressed here straight on but rather, we might say, sideways. Hopefully, however, my focus here on the theme of suffering does not distort the more obvious themes in Paul but rather broadens their significance.

this we will move on to examining Paul's thought on suffering using our previously established categories. For in Romans not only is Paul concerned about humanity as a whole in regard to suffering but, because of his conviction that a radically new situation has been created in Christ, he also distinguishes between the suffering of those who believe in Christ and those who do not.[2]

Humanity's Shared Suffering

In Romans Paul turns his gaze toward suffering's broad sweep: believers and nonbelievers, as well as all creation, groan in this time.[3] This present time is one of suffering (8:18),[4] and that is because sin roams the

2. In examining 1 Thessalonians and Philippians I started with the suffering of believers since that most accurately reflected Paul's concentration in those letters. Romans is somewhat different. Paul's concern for the plight of all humanity, while it may have been implicit in those other letters, is explicit in Romans. As any reader of Romans knows, Paul begins this letter by focusing his hearers' attention on the dilemma of those who do not believe. Consequently, after discussing suffering as the common lot of humanity I will turn not to the suffering of believers, as I did with the his other letters, but to that of nonbelievers.

3. I take the reference to κτίσις in 8:22 to be to all that is, humanity and non-human creation. So also E. Käsemann, *Commentary on Romans*, tr. and ed. G. W. Bromiley (Grand Rapids: Eerdmans, 1980), p. 233; J. G. Gibbs, *Creation and Redemption: A Study in Pauline Theology* (Leiden: Brill, 1971), p. 40. Paul's words in 8:23 — "even we ourselves..." — do not suggest that he sees believers as separate from the rest of creation. They serve rather to clarify that he holds the opposite view.

4. While the reference to παθήμα in 8:18, coming as it does right after Paul speaks of συμπάσχομεν — in context; "suffering with Christ" (8:17) — requires that we understand him to be including the suffering of believers here, it does not require that we understand him to be referring *only* to the suffering of believers, as several commentators would argue (C. E. B. Cranfield, *The Epistle to the Romans* [International Critical Commentary; Edinburgh: Clark, 1975], I, p. 409; J. D. G. Dunn, *Romans* [Word Biblical Commentary; Dallas: Word, 1988], p. 468; P. Stuhlmacher, *Paul's Letter to the Romans: A Commentary*, tr. S. J. Hafemann [Louisville: Westminster John Knox, 1994], p. 133). Since Paul goes on to say that the whole creation is groaning, Käsemann is correct that here Paul "unites cosmic and Christian suffering" (*Romans*, p. 232). See also A. Gieniusz, *Romans 8:18-30: "Suffering Does Not Thwart the Future Glory"* (Atlanta: Scholars, 1999), pp. 213-14.

world. Paul lets his Scripture say it for him: "none is righteous, no, not one" (3:10).

Sin Is a Power That Causes Suffering

In Romans sin is not primarily transgression of either the Torah or a moral law, although it is that.[5] Sin is rather a power, and, Paul says, humans are "under it" (3:9). For Paul sin chiefly "means, in almost hypostasizing fashion, the power of sin."[6] Paul's intense focus on this power is rooted not in moral distaste so much as in his profound concern for humanity's troubles.

His conviction is that sin causes suffering's presence in human life.[7] As W. Grundmann puts it: for Paul "sin is the author of all evil."[8] Suffering's root is sin — "unrighteousness"[9] — and unfortunately, both believers and nonbelievers are caught in this destructive force. Sin has a virulent capacity to spread itself through vicious human interaction[10] and by unsettling individuals' minds and beings.[11] Sin's lethal association with both believers and nonbelievers means that all humanity suffers.

Sin is the root of human suffering — whether the darkness of phys-

---

5. The word "sin" appears in the plural ("sins") referring to sinful acts only three times in Romans: 4:7; 7:5; and 11:27. Singular "sin" refers to sinful actions in 5:20. And see 1:24-32, which includes a list of actions that go against "God's decree."

6. Käsemann, *Romans,* p. 86. J. L. Martyn, whose important commentary on Galatians is dedicated to Käsemann, indicates Paul's thought by capitalizing the word: "Sin" in Romans is "a cosmic power" (*Galatians* [New York: Doubleday, 1997], p. 372). Cf. I. de la Potterie and S. Lyonnet: *"hamartia* (is) evil power personified" (*The Christian Lives by the Spirit* [New York: Alba, 1971], p. 155).

7. So also E. Tamez, *The Amnesty of Grace: Justification by Faith from a Latin American Perspective,* tr. S. H. Ringe (Nashville: Abingdon, 1993), p. 116.

8. ἁμαρτάνω, in *Theological Dictionary of the New Testament,* ed. G. Kittel, tr. G. W. Bromiley (Grand Rapids: Eerdmans, 1964), I, pp. 302-16, here p. 309.

9. As for Paul the opposite of sin is righteousness (6:18), sin and unrighteousness are for him one and the same.

10. Rom 1:24-31.

11. Below I will argue for this on the basis of chs. 7 and 9–11.

ical death or the destructive experiences of our existence. The power of sin seeks to destroy life, and so its closest ally is physical death (5:12). Paul is convinced that sin and death are inseparable. Because there is sin, there is death. In other words, death is not a natural event but a punishment for sin (1:32).[12]

The power of sin trades in instruments of decay, which include disease and natural disasters. Turmoils of illness[13] and natural calamities[14] are evidence of sin's capacity and concern to destroy God's good creation. (That Paul considers sin as the root of all disorders, including disease, although he does not name this category of suffering, is not to be confused with the idea that would blame an individual person's illness on that individual's sin.) R. Jewett rightly interprets Paul's reference to "decay" — "creation itself will be set free from its bondage to decay" (8:21) — as (in modern terms) a recognition that ecological disorder is one of the results of sin.[15] Put another way, "creation is affected by [human] action . . . [it] bears the pain of the Fall."[16] Jewett further recognizes, along with others,[17] that in this Paul echoes the Jewish view that sin corrupts not just humanity but also God's creation.[18] The sufferings that come from disorders, whether of body or of nature, are signs of creation's subjugation to

12. This view of death as unnatural has, of course, logical and theological problems. See comments by R. W. Jenson, *Systematic Theology* II: *The Works of God* (Oxford: Oxford University Press, 1999), pp. 330-31.

13. That Paul considers sin the root of all disorders, including disease (although he does not name this category of suffering), is not to be confused with the idea that would blame an individual person's illness on that individual's sin.

14. Paul's reference to "famine" as one of the sufferings that seeks to separate believers from God's love (8:35) indicates his recognition that sin makes itself felt through disasters of nature.

15. R. Jewett, *Romans: A Commentary* (Hermeneia; Minneapolis: Fortress, 2006), pp. 513-15. See also M. D. Baker and J. R. Wagner, "The Righteousness of God and Hurricane Mitch: Reading Romans in Hurricane-Devastated Honduras," in *Navigating Romans Through Cultures*, ed. Yeo Khiok-khng (New York: Clark, 2004), pp. 95-132, here p. 111.

16. Gibbs, *Creation and Redemption*, p. 40. Cf. B. Bryne, *Romans* (Sacra Pagina; Collegeville: Liturgical, 1996), p. 259.

17. E.g., Käsemann, *Romans*, p. 233.

18. Jewett, *Romans*, pp. 512-15.

sin, which holds it in a state of perishability,[19] depriving it of God's intention for it, which is incorruptibility. While it is God who has now subjected creation to decay (presumably, in Paul's mind a reflection of God's curse on the ground in Gen 3:17),[20] God did so in hope (8:20), that is, as L. Keck puts it, "with an eye to its eventual liberation and participation in the same future that God's children will enjoy."[21] The current state of affairs in creation is against God's overarching will for it. What now obtains is the result of sin.

Put bluntly, sin's agenda is to put out the light and life of God. This may be perceived as rather Manichaean, as if Paul thought there were two cosmic contenders at war with each other — God and Sin. Strange as it may sound, there is something to this perception. Not that Paul was a Manichaean, but that he viewed sin as a force greater than the human will, a force whose raison d'être is to defeat God's will. At the same time, Paul is never uncertain about who is in control of the cosmos. God is and always has been in charge, and God is and always has been directing creation toward ultimate freedom from sin.[22]

It must be emphasized that sin, the producer of suffering, is not simply some foreign entity that we humans can shake our finger at and blame for our troubles. Paul understands sin as a power beyond our control, a force greater than us, but also as a part of our very beings. Humans are shaped by sin so that we either willingly or unwittingly cooperate with it. In the course of that cooperation we contribute to our own and other people's sufferings. This is the case whether or not we are believers.

---

19. See T. Holtz on Rom 8:21 regarding φθορά as "perishability" (*Exegetical Dictionary of the New Testament*, ed. H. Balz and G. Schneider [Grand Rapids: Eerdmans, 1993], III, p. 423).

20. So Cranfield, *Romans*, I, p. 414.

21. *Romans* (Abingdon New Testament Commentaries; Nashville: Abingdon, 2005), p. 211.

22. This understanding accords with Martyn's apocalyptic understanding of Paul; Paul believed that "there are genuine powers arrayed against God, yet ultimately subject to God's sovereignty" (*Galatians*, p. 373; see also pp. 97-105).

Believers and Nonbelievers Have
Distinct Relationships to Sin

It is important to notice at this juncture that for Paul sin has an association with believers that is distinct from what it has with nonbelievers: sin completely masters nonbelievers;[23] believers, on the other hand, are shaped by the wounds we bear from our former bondage (7:14)[24] so that we are still drawn to sin while no longer being indentured to it.

Yet, despite the difference between sin's claim on those who believe and its claim on those who do not, Paul understands all humans as either captive (unbelievers) or captivated (believers) by sin. As a result, suffering and death are the common lot of humanity.

Human Suffering in the Present

Paul opens Romans with the declaration that the wrath of God is being revealed against all human ungodliness and unrighteousness (1:18).[25] His description of some of the symptoms of this ungodliness and unrighteousness — moronic thinking (1:22), uncleanness (1:24), "dishonor-

---

23. While Paul's words in 2:6-7 are often taken to refer to nonbelievers (so E. P. Sanders, *Paul, the Law and the Jewish People* [Philadelphia: Fortress, 1983], pp. 123-24), it is to be noted that his reference to these people seeking for glory and honor and incorruptibility as they do good indicates that he regards their good actions as expressions of faith (cf. Cranfield, *Romans*, I, p. 147). Of course, Paul is not talking here about believers in Christ but about people operating on the basis of faith (cf. D. B. Garlington, *Faith, Obedience, and Perseverance: Aspects of Paul's Letter to the Romans* [Tübingen: Mohr, 1994], p. 68). Käsemann notes that here Paul commends obedience (*Romans*, p. 60), and we note that for Paul obedience is a synonym for faith. Calvin takes it that Paul is speaking here of "the faithful" (*Commentaries on The Epistle of Paul the Apostle to the Romans*, tr. J. Owen [Grand Rapids: Eerdmans, 1948], p. 90).

24. I will argue below for this reading.

25. Paul's description of ungodliness here is not to a past stage of human life nor to a particular society but, as Cranfield wisely notes, to "the innermost truth of all of us." This passage "depicts man as he appears in the light of the cross of Christ" (*Romans*, I, p. 104).

ing of their bodies among themselves" (1:24), dishonorable passions (1:26), base minds (1:28), "every kind of wickedness, evil, covetousness," etc. (1:29; see 1:29-31) — details not just the fruits of unrighteousness but the seeds of suffering.

While Paul blames this particular sorry summary of social violence on unbelief in God, by the time we read his words in ch. 2 regarding Jews (who acknowledge God and God's law, while stealing, committing adultery, and the like, 2:17-24), we see that Paul thinks that everyone who does not believe in Christ, whether Jew or Gentile, perpetuates and is subjected to these troubles. And, by the time we read Romans 7 (which I will argue refers to the believer in Christ), it seems evident that Paul thinks that all people, whether or not they believe in Christ, practice evil (7:19).

For Paul, both believers and nonbelievers undergo and trade in the troubles that attend human existence: being victims and perpetrators of social violence, experiencing the terror and loss of the decay that shrouds creation, facing physical death, and, as we shall shortly see, struggling with existential anguish. Believers and nonbelievers, then, share similarities in our present — we are both dazzled and daunted by sin's muscle. Although the nature of sin's claim on us is different, unfortunately both believers and nonbelievers find our common enemy magnetic, and so we suffer and cause suffering.

Beyond the blatant manifestations of sin's destructiveness summarized in the various forms of sufferings described above, there is also a more subtle manifestation of sin's destructiveness. Sin's magnetism has a capacity to draw our eyes toward our own definition of reality and away from God's, to turn us inward and blinker our eyes to God's faithfulness, to draw us away from faith in God and so to ask of ourselves that we be God. As Käsemann says, sin "is the human attempt to rob God of his power."[26]

26. *Romans,* pp. 89-90.

The Suffering of Lack of Trust in God's Righteousness

Both believers and nonbelievers are susceptible to the delusions that sin engenders and so to the resultant existential misery of blaming God and of relying on ourselves. Both believers and nonbelievers may be blinded to God's trustworthiness and so choose to live in the shadow of our definitions of God and ourselves rather than in the light of faith.

In Romans 9–11 Paul describes this wretchedness. His description ostensibly concerns "unsaved" fellow Jews (10:1) but, as we shall see, it actually concerns us all. Jews, Paul says, who are ignorant of the righteousness that comes from God (10:3), having not recognized the Christ (9:5), are guilty of trespass (11:11-12) and disobedience (11:31; cf. 10:21), which is to say, unbelief.[27] Paul understands his kinsfolk's lack of faith to be a sign of sin and a result of their slavery to it.[28]

In these chapters of Romans Paul creates a conversation between Israel and God in which he reflects his understanding of Israel's long-standing "disobedience" (10:21) or lack of trust in God. The density of scriptural citations in these chapters serves in part the purpose of dramatizing the struggle between Israel and God[29] — Israel wanting to live according to her understanding of justice and righteousness, relying on

27. As Rom 1:5 indicates, for Paul faith and obedience are tautological, therefore so are disobedience and unbelief. The ambiguous grammar of the phrase "obedience of faith" (1:5) has produced a variety of readings. D. B. Garlington notes that there are really only two viable options: the obedience that is faith or the obedience that proceeds from faith. These two options say the same thing while placing different emphases on the organically connected decision of faith and response to faith (*"The Obedience of Faith": A Pauline Phrase in Historical Context* [Tübingen: Mohr, 1991], p. 1, n. 4). That is, Paul regards obedience as a synonym for faith and disobedience as a synonym for unbelief.

28. When Paul says in 11:32 that God has consigned all to disobedience, he is saying something similar to what he said earlier — that God has handed over to sinning all who do not acknowledge him (1:24). Obedience and faith, being one and the same thing (1:5), are, in Paul's terms, the means and the result of being freed from sin. Disobedience and unbelief are, then, the means and the result of being servants of sin.

29. See S. K. Stowers for how in portions of Romans 9–11 Paul utilizes Scripture to create the debate between false and correct understandings of God's faithfulness (*The Diatribe and Paul's Letter to the Romans* [Society of Biblical Literature Dissertation Series 57; Chico: Scholars, 1981], p. 121).

her own capacities, and God, through the Scriptures, reminding Israel that God's ways alone should be her ways.

Believers' Lack of Trust

In chs. 9–11 Paul addresses believers and speaks about nonbelievers.[30] That he devotes a good portion of a letter written to people who believe in Christ[31] dramatizing the struggle of those who do not believe (Israel) strongly suggests that he expects his words about nonbelieving Jews to be pertinent to his Roman audience. This is made more obvious by his occasional eyeballing of his converted audience (e.g., 10:1; 11:13, 19, 25).[32] Paul's description in Romans 9–11, then, serves both to express his anguish and hope for "unsaved" Jews and to exhort all who do believe.

His intensity in chs. 9–11, meant to clear his hearers' hearts of conceit (11:25) by clarifying for them that they have not displaced Israel in God's purposes[33] — for God's faithfulness is sure, is at once a call to trust God. It is another line in the rich counterpoint of Romans on the theme of faith in God through Jesus Christ.

---

30. Cf. P. Meyer, "Romans 10:4 and the End of the Law," in *The Divine Helmsman: Studies on God's Control of Human Events Presented to Lou H. Silberman*, ed. J. L. Crenshaw and S. Sandmel (New York: Ktav, 1980), pp. 59-79, here p. 71; S. K. Stowers, *A Rereading of Romans: Justice, Jews, and Gentiles* (New Haven: Yale University Press, 1994), p. 291; also, Käsemann's recognition that here Paul links salvation history to the doctrine of justification (*Romans*, p. 317) acknowledges that this is addressed to believers while speaking about nonbelievers.

31. In all probability, Paul's addressees are both Gentile (11:13) and Jew (15:7-12). See Cranfield on the composition of the Roman church (*Romans*, I). There is an extensive scholarly discussion on the issue of the ethnic complexion of the Roman believers.

32. It is difficult to know if the address in 9:19 is to a real or imaginary interlocutor (so Cranfield, *Romans*, II, p. 489). Whoever it is, it most likely expresses the Jewish point of view and not that of Paul's converted audience (cf. Dunn, *Romans*, p. 555), although Stowers sees it both as an address to an imaginary interlocutor and as a "form of censure for the addressees of the letter" (*Diatribe*, p. 114).

33. Cf. Cranfield: "It is only where the Church persists in refusing to learn (that it is by God's mercy alone that it lives), where it . . . believes that its own existence is based on human achievement, and so fails to understand God's mercy to itself, that it is unable to believe in God's mercy for still unbelieving Israel" (*Romans*, II, p. 448).

Here Paul again calls believers to have faith in God's righteousness as revealed in Christ. He does this, as I have said, by describing the situation of those who do not believe (10:1-4) and, as we shall see, by facing head-on the most challenging obstacle to trust in God's righteousness: the fact that Gentiles and not God's people Israel predominate "in" Israel's Christ. As readers of Romans have often noted, one of Paul's chief foci in this letter and especially in chs. 9–11 is to defend the faithfulness of God to God's election of Israel, what Keck termed the "moral integrity of God."[34]

In chs. 9–11 Paul seeks to make believers aware of our propensity, which we share with the rest of humanity, to blame God and trust in our own capacities as if we owned ourselves. In doing this Paul endeavors to help believers, and through believers all humanity, to escape an experience of living tinged by angst and doubt and the futile desire to control our lives and create our own forms of justice apart from the only justice there is — that of God. Paul's worry is that believers readily succumb to the comfort of our own versions of reality, of our place in it, and of what constitutes right and wrong and as a result limit God's trustworthiness/righteousness to our own categories (11:25). When we do this, we, like the rest of humanity, are subject to the useless and tormenting exercise of trying to be our own God. Reading these chapters, Luther puts it that Paul invites his readers into a life which, by being based on faith is freed of sin's dominance so that "the believer is afraid of nothing, but stands quiet and secure on a firm rock."[35]

While the struggle Paul portrays in Romans 9–11 is, in the first instance, only *Israel's*, it is also that of *believers in the Christ.* Moreover, it is also, as I will directly argue, the struggle of *all unbelievers,* whether Jew or Gentile.

---

34. Quoted from R. B. Hays, *Echoes of Scripture in the Letters of Paul* (New Haven: Yale University Press, 1989), p. 47. Hays himself is among those who regard Paul's focus in Romans to be the defense of God's faithfulness in light of the rejection of the gospel by most Jews and its acceptance by many Gentiles.

35. *Romans,* p. 144.

Nonbelievers' Lack of Trust

If trust in God's righteousness, which is the only way to view things aright and to dispel sin's delusions, is a challenge for those who are "in" Christ, Paul regards delusion as the state of things for those apart from Christ. Paul diagnoses the lives of nonbelieving Jews and Gentiles as full of striving and complaint, lacking the peace that comes from faith (cf. 5:1).[36] As we have seen, he does this while holding this diagnosis in front of the noses of believers, hoping that we may recognize these same symptoms in ourselves.

"Unsaved" Israel (10:1) is here representative of all humanity who have not believed in Christ.[37] Israel's call is to be God's representative of how humanity should and could live — a light for the nations.[38] Those of Israel who now resist the Christ are in respect to that call as if they were no longer God's people.[39] In other words, they are now as if they were the "nations," the Gentiles. Israel's lack of faith in God's Christ is the epitome of the unbelief exhibited also by Gentiles (cf. 11:32).

Paul's claim that God makes no distinction between Jew and Greek who call upon him in faith (10:12) works also the other way round. The Jews' special place in God's purposes for the whole world becomes, for those Jews who do not believe, the place of representing all *unbelievers,* whether Jew or Greek. The disobedience of the Jews has its own

36. This peace is more than an "inner peace"; it is, as 5:1-11 indicates, the peace known subsequent to having been God's enemies; it is the peace of companionship with God.

37. Cf. Käsemann, *Romans,* p. 311.

38. Implied in 15:8-9.

39. A. K. Grieb comments on this passage: "Paul is clear that salvation happens only in Jesus Christ" (*The Story of Romans: A Narrative Defense of God's Righteousness* [Louisville: Westminster John Knox, 2002], p. 96). Of course, many scholars of Paul have been careful not to read him this way. Paul, it is argued, thought that Christ came for the Gentiles. This did not change the fact that the Jews' salvation would be based, as it always had been, on the law. See, e.g., Stowers, *Rereading Romans,* p. 308. For a description of this "two ways" reading of Paul's soteriology, see J. G. Gager, *Reinventing Paul* (Oxford: Oxford University Press, 2000), pp. 57-75.

uniqueness — it serves a purpose on behalf of Gentiles (11:28-31) while at the same time being paradigmatic for all humanity's lack of faith.

Why God Can Be Trusted and Why
Such Trust Alleviates Our Anguish

I have suggested that Romans 9–11 describes difficulties encountered by both believers and nonbelievers. In these chapters Paul calls attention to the elephant in the room — the question of God's faithfulness and justice.[40] He asks both believers and nonbelievers to face the elephant. In the course of concentrating on this large and potentially destructive concern, Paul affirms that God has not changed God's mind with respect to Israel — the gifts and the call of God are irrevocable (11:29) — and that God's mercy, not our sense of justice, has always defined God's relationship to God's people. In other words, God's freedom to have compassion on whom God will have compassion (9:15) is at once God's righteousness.

In order to have a peaceful relationship with this righteous and free God (which is the same as living with reality as it is) we humans must not rely on either our own sense of justice or on our ability to enact justice, but only on our trust in God.[41] Paul admonishes

---

40. Cf. R. B. Hays: "the purpose of Romans 9–11 . . . is to show that God's dealing with Israel and the nations in the present age is fully consistent with God's modus operandi in the past and with his declared purposes" (*Echoes of Scripture,* p. 64).

41. These chapters have a history of interpretation which allows Paul's reference to election and predestination to predominate (for a historical survey of this line of interpretation, see W. Sanday and A. Headlam, *The Epistle to the Romans* [International Critical Commentary; Edinburgh: Clark, 1895], pp. 269-75). There is, as other readers of these chapters have noted, another theme which arguably eclipses that of predestination — that of God's mercy (so Cranfield, *Romans,* II, pp. 448, 472). By the end of ch. 11, Paul has declared his conviction — despite his earlier splitting of Israel into the remnant and those who remain disobedient — that *all* Israel will be saved. See Fitzmyer's understanding regarding Paul's use of "Israel": these chapters culminate in an understanding that "the Jewish people as a whole, both 'the remnant' (11:5) . . . and 'the others' (11:7), will be saved" (*Romans* [Anchor Bible; New York: Doubleday, 1992], p. 623). Paul's overarching theme is, then, not predestination but, in Käsemann's words "the miracle of grace which transforms the ungodly" (*Romans,* p. 274).

humanity[42] for thinking God unjust when God chooses the younger over the elder (9:12-14) even before either have had a chance to prove themselves capable of good or bad actions (9:11). This reaction to God's ways is instinctual to humanity, whether of the "saved" or the "not saved" variety. It judges God on our terms instead of learning to live with God as God is.[43] This reaction to God resists the glory God offers us and clings instead to our human horizons.

Clearly, the matter of God's faithfulness is an existential and not an academic one for Paul (see 9:1-3). Given his conviction that trust in God is the bedrock of life (1:17),[44] Paul both addresses the doubt capable of shaking that foundation (the conversion of Gentiles and the rejection of the gospel by the Jews) and describes the existential anguish that attends the striving to establish our own version of righteousness rather than trusting in God's righteousness (whether we do not believe in Christ or do).

For Paul, without faith in God's righteousness, without trust in God's trustworthy character, life is a misery. When we cannot trust God, the only alternative is to blame God for being unjust (9:14), to live in a state of resistance to God. It is only when we believe in God's righteousness that we can live with God's freedom to say: "I will have mercy on whom I have mercy, and I will have compassion on whom I have compassion" (9:15). Trust in God alone allows recognition that those things that appear counterintuitive (that we cannot establish our own righteousness, 10:3) and ostensibly unjust ("Jacob I loved, but Esau I hated," 9:13) appear so because we — whether believers or not — have lost our focus on God. Only faith in God's trustworthiness and righ-

---

42. Again, this is addressed to believers in Christ while describing, from a believer's perspective, the dilemma of nonbelievers in Christ.

43. Cf. Luther's words referring to the summary statement in 11:32: "Take to heart this great text. By it the whole righteousness of the world and of man is damned: by it the righteousness of God is alone exalted, the righteousness of God which is by faith" (cited in K. Barth, *The Epistle to the Romans*, tr. E. C. Hoskyns [London: Oxford, 1933], p. 421).

44. Life for Paul is, of course, more than existing and breathing; it is living out of God's life — the only life there is.

teousness, only acceptance of God's character as wholly good, only a craving for God's glory, gives humanity the right eyes and ears with which to deal with human existence as created by God.

Paul recognizes that the challenge for humanity of living not toward ourselves but toward God extends to acknowledging the limits of our understanding instead of applying our standards of justice to ourselves and others. This challenge, in other words, is to trust God while saying along with Paul, "how unsearchable are [God's] judgments and how inscrutable are his ways" (11:33). It is the challenge of accepting the good news: that God's saving power is available to all who believe in God's righteousness and not in our own; that righteousness and life come from faith and not from our striving.

This challenge stands before not only nonbelievers but also believers. In short, it is the ongoing struggle of every person.

A History of Suffering

Paul judges all humankind to have a history shaped by sin and so by suffering. In Rom 1:24-32 he details this sorry past — a past which is nonbelievers' present and which still affects believers.

Suffering in the Future

Not only do believers share with nonbelievers a history of slavery to sin, making us participants in the same legacy of perpetuating suffering as nonbelievers, but believers share, at least in the short term, a common future with those who do not believe in Jesus Christ. Both our bodies and those of nonbelievers will die. So now, even though we believers have been liberated from sin's mastery, in K. Barth's words, we nevertheless "see all men doing what Adam did, and then suffering as Adam suffered. We see men sin, and then die."[45]

45. *Romans*, p. 172.

There is no question in Paul's mind but that physical death is a form of suffering.[46] His enthusiastic cry that death's rule has ended with Christ (5:17) works on the presumption that all would see this as good news, that humanity shares in common a horrifying fear of physical death. Paul's declaration is a sound of joy in response to what he presumes all people feel — that the death of our bodies is a profound form of suffering.

Believers' liberation from sin unfortunately does not completely wipe out the past from our present — we still die because of sin (8:10).[47] We believers may be able to hope for a future life for our bodies (8:11),[48] but now both we and those who do not share our faith share the same fate: our physical bodies die.

Our bodies, just like all bodies, are affected by sin and consequently will know the suffering of death. Calvin writes concerning the Christian: "the price of our redemption was paid by Christ, but in such a way that death still holds us in its chains."[49] Paul's claim that those "in Christ" are released from both the power of sin and the finality of death does not obliterate his admission that this liberation is more inaugurated than complete. We believers must wait for the future when our bodies will be made alive.

46. This he, of course, shares in common with his Jewish kinsfolk. See H. W. Wolff, *Anthropology of the Old Testament* (Philadelphia: Fortress, 1974), p. 102. Cf. Barth, who reads Paul as speaking of death as "the supreme tribulation in which we stand. . . . we try . . . to protect our eyes against the grey light of the final negation which envelops all our healthy, creative, positive activities . . . if there be salvation, it must be salvation from death" (*Romans*, pp. 166-67).

47. Cf. Cranfield; "the Christian must still submit to death as the wages of sin, because he is a sinner" (*Romans*, I, p. 389).

48. Calvin thinks that in this verse Paul is referring to "the continued working of the Spirit by which he gradually mortifies the relics of the flesh" (*Romans*, p. 293), but Fitzmyer rightly notes, on the basis both of the future tense and of the phrase "mortal body," that Paul is referring to something other than "the body of death" (e.g., 7:24), from which believers can now be gradually liberated. Paul is referring rather to the eschatological resurrection of Christians (*Romans*, p. 491; see also Dunn, *Romans*, p. 445).

49. *The Epistles of Paul the Apostle to the Romans and to the Thessalonians*, tr. R. Mackenzie (Grand Rapids: Eerdmans, 1960), pp. 175-76.

Suffering as Humans "in Christ"

I have alluded to Paul's understanding that, in terms of relationship to sin, there is a distinction between believers and nonbelievers. Put simply, Paul considers that believers are no longer dominated by sin, although we are influenced by it, whereas nonbelievers remain imprisoned by sin.

Shortly, when we turn to the section on the suffering of nonbelievers, we will discuss Paul's understanding of the consequences of nonbelievers' servitude to sin. Before proceeding, it is important to note that Paul thinks that that portion of humanity that believes in Christ may experience human afflictions in a unique context — the context of being "in Christ." Paul regards believers as having the possibility of a believing-specific experience of the inescapable sufferings that we, like nonbelievers, know. I will term this "in Christ" suffering. Later, in the section on the suffering of believers I will focus both on this "in Christ" suffering and on the suffering believers take on by believing in Christ. This will be termed "with Christ" suffering.

Suffering of Nonbelievers

Nonbelievers, Indentured to Sin, Help Spread Suffering

Paul's analysis is that those who do not believe in God, or in Jesus Christ, know and cause suffering (as do believers, as we shall see).

Sin's defeat is signaled in Christ's resurrection; the alleviation of all suffering began when *Christ's* suffering was alleviated. At his resurrection from the dead Christ overcame the ultimate suffering. Consequently, Paul is convinced that unless humanity participates in Christ's death (6:3) we will not be able to participate in the justice (righteousness) that opposes and heals suffering. For Christ's death, ending in life, is the only means by which sin and suffering and physical death can be obliterated. Paul thinks that those outside Christ, those who are not baptized into Christ's death (6:4), are left utterly exposed to the manipulations of sin, which always produce suffering. Unlike believers, who are not required to live as "debtors to the flesh" (8:12), those apart from Christ think they owe their lives to that very sphere that brings death (8:12).

Paul's conviction is that the only possibility for facing down sin's power is from the context of being "in Christ." Humans may share the righteousness of Christ through believing in Christ and so, on the basis of Christ's righteousness, may have the capacity to resist sin.[50] Only those who have faith in Christ and so are "in Christ" the righteous one have a shield against sin's force. Paul even considers his fellow Jews to be under sin's power (3:9).

It is God's righteousness alone, apart from the law, that holds what humanity craves — freedom from suffering. For God's righteousness is not only the opposite of sin but also the antidote to its vicious hold on humanity. Only God's righteousness, as manifested apart from the law and through belief in Jesus Christ (3:21-22),[51] can make humans righteous. And consequently, God's righteousness is the only solution to the sorry state of suffering that humankind endures.

The good news of Christ is the good news that God's power is at work for the purpose of saving (1:16), of creating the opportunity for humanity to know freedom from suffering, which freedom was God's original intent.[52] Those who reject this good news thus bring about their own and other people's sufferings. (As we will see, for Paul even those who *do* accept the good news unfortunately continue to trade in unrighteousness.) Paul is convinced that only by participation in God's righteousness may the world's ills be cured.

Paul cares intensely that all the world become accountable to the

---

50. Cf. Luther: "the righteousness of Christ becomes his who believes on Him; and the sin of him who believes on Him becomes that of Christ. Therefore sin cannot remain on him who believes, just as man's sin could not remain on Christ" (*Commentary on the Epistle to the Romans*, tr. J. T. Mueller [Grand Rapids: Kregel, 1954], p. 144).

51. The debate over whether Paul refers to Christ's faithfulness in 3:22 (the subjective genitive reading) is not germane here.

52. Cf. Byrne, who understands Paul's gospel as sharing with the Jewish apocalyptic worldview the idea of salvation "as the arrival at that fullness of life and humanity which fulfills the Creator's original design for human beings, created in the image and likeness of God" (*Romans*, p. 51).

one who holds the key to a world healed (3:19). Such accountability will, in Paul's view, restore humanity to its intended glory, reflecting the character of the one whose only goal is love and harmony. Belief in God, the one who raised Jesus from the dead, allows humans to become righteous (4:24-25) and so to participate in combating all that is not righteous — all that causes pain and suffering. As Augustine recognized, for Paul when sin dies, justice rises.[53]

Paul regards God as the just judge (3:5-7) who stands against all that is unrighteous, that is, against the torments that humans inflict on each other and themselves. Those who choose not to acknowledge this God are in effect perpetuating humanity's woes. This is so, in Paul's view, because those who would snub God are still enslaved to sin — the source of all suffering.

The Suffering of Those Who Do Not Believe in God

Initially in Romans Paul divides the unconverted into two groups in relation to suffering's source — sin. First he addresses those who do not acknowledge God, and then he turns to those who know God but do not believe in Jesus Christ.

Paul's depiction of the suffering that people who do not acknowledge God experience and cause is given early in the letter (1:18-31): such people are perpetrators and victims of murder, gossip, heartlessness, and so on.[54] Choosing to ignore God results in the darkness and difficulties that humans experience among themselves (1:24). While some do practice goodness (2:7), the human dilemma is such that sin so dominates the human will (3:9) that humanity lives in a state overwhelmed by suffering.

Paul then turns to Jews, who acknowledge God but not Jesus as the Christ. Paul regards the dictates of the Jews' law as inhibitors to human

---

53. Augustine comments on 4:25: "in his being handed over sin is mentioned; in his resurrection justice is mentioned. Therefore let sin die, and let justice rise" (*Sermon* 236.1, quoted by Fitzmyer, *Romans*, p. 390).

54. I have noted above that this record of unrighteousness is neither time nor culture bound. It is Paul's description of humanity with its back turned to God.

suffering, for these dictates require people not to steal from each other, not to commit adultery, and so on (2:21-23). God's righteousness, as described for humans to emulate in the law, is focused on reducing, even abolishing, the sufferings that humans inflict on each other. The law allows people to recognize and identify the root of suffering — sin (3:20). However, the law is not powerful enough on its own to quash sin. And neither are human beings. Suffering's source is too devious and pervasive for any other than God to stop it.

And so faith is the key to meeting the challenge of sin. Trust in God, the only one stronger than sin, is the one and only option for those who desire freedom from sin, which is the same as righteousness. Faith has always been the context for the Jews' relationship with God,[55] but, Paul charges, his fellow Jews have ignored this and instead have tried to follow the law without faith (9:32).

Paul claims that Christ, who became a servant to the Jews in order to confirm God's promises to them (15:8), is for the Jews the manifestation of God's faithfulness to them. It is because God is trustworthy and true (15:8) that the good news in Jesus Christ is first for the Jews (1:16). That Paul's kinsfolk have not trusted in God's faithfulness to them in Christ grieves Paul to his very core (9:2).[56]

---

55. The contribution of the "new perspective on Paul" initiated by E. P. Sanders *(Paul and Palestininan Judaism)* is the recognition on the part of mainly non-Jewish biblical scholars that Jews understood following the law as a grateful response to God's saving action and that Paul's critique of Judaism could not therefore have been that law observance was "legalistic." "New perspective" scholars disagree over what it was that Paul found wrong with Judaism or whether he was even concerned about Judaism (as opposed to Jewish believers in Christ and their desire to require Gentiles to follow the law). This large area of debate is tangential to our investigation here. What may be claimed without argument and in agreement with the "new perspective" is that Paul's problem is not with the law itself but with the manner in which it is observed: it needs to be carried out in the context of faith. The highly contentious issue of whether for Jews that faith needs to include acceptance that Jesus is the Christ cannot occupy our time in this inquiry. I have already signaled my disagreement with the "two ways" reading of Paul's soteriology.

56. S. Westerholm's "Lutheran" reading of this passage is convincing: "Jews continue to pursue righteousness through . . . works (9:32); this pursuit Paul finds misguided, not because the law does not demand works . . . , but because no one *is* righ-

As we saw in the section on humanity's shared suffering, Paul's concern about his fellow Jews being liberated from sin's grip is not only for the sake of their future salvation but also for the sake of their understanding the ways of God in the midst of the trials of living. Without faith, life is a constant struggle with God, full of complaint and striving and deep-seated anxiety, as Paul dramatizes with his Scripture-saturated discourse in 9:6–11:10.

Paul's burning desire for his fellow Jews (and for all humanity)[57] is that they turn their beings in trust toward the God who longs to save them from sin's insatiable desire to use them (and us) for its own destructive purposes.

It is to be noted that Paul is firmly convinced that his desire will be fulfilled (11:26).

Nonbelievers, Whether Jew or Gentile, Create Suffering

In the end, Paul forgoes his distinction of Gentiles and Jews in regard to the dilemma they face and perpetuate. Since all except those "in Christ" are subject to sin rather than righteousness, in Paul's view all nonbelievers, whether Gentile or Jew, cooperate with sin and so help to proliferate suffering. Paul's judgment is that in the paths of all who do not believe in Jesus Christ lie "ruin and misery" (3:16).

Nonbelievers, Whether Jew or Gentile, Will Suffer

Moreover, nonbelievers live under the burden of condemnation (8:1). The only future open to those who reject God's offer of freedom from

---

teous, and God has provided for the righteousness of sinners, through Christ, by faith. Justification is thus a gift of grace, received through faith, not gained by works" (*Perspectives Old and New on Paul: The "Lutheran" Paul and His Critics* [Grand Rapids: Eerdmans, 2004], p. 400).

57. It is to be remembered that I argued above that for Paul unbelieving Jews are representative of all unbelievers.

sin, God's invitation to know God's glory, is wrath (5:9). Nonbelievers, as slaves of sin, suffer under the shadow of death and of God's wrath.

Nonbelievers, Whether Jew or Gentile, Will Be Subject to God's Wrath

Despite overwhelming evidence of the strength of sin to reach its tentacles into human life through every form of "ruin and misery," Paul's astonishing conviction is that the opposite of sin — righteousness — will triumph (2:5; cf. 3:5-6) and so suffering's term will be ended. Suffering will be ended, that is, for all except those who choose cooperation with sin rather than repentance. If people choose unrighteousness, they will know God's wrath.

Paul is convinced, then, that not only do nonbelievers experience and cause suffering now, but they are "storing up wrath" for themselves (2:5). People who participate in perpetuating suffering in this world, that is, people who remain under sin's mastery, will receive extra suffering when God's wrath is revealed in its furious fullness (2:8). Paul promises "tribulation and anguish" for all who refuse to be liberated from sin, whether Jew or Gentile (2:9).

The Suffering of Believers: Suffering "in Christ" and "with Christ"

Believers, according to Paul, experience suffering both as humans living in this time when sin's capacity is still vigorous and because they believe in Christ. We may for our purposes here distinguish these sufferings by understanding one as "in Christ" and the other as "with Christ."[58]

In regard to the first, it is clear that believers, like nonbelievers, experience suffering — the effects of sin. However, believers experience

58. The distinction I am making here is heuristic. Paul himself does not use these categories in distinguishing aspects of believers' suffering.

such suffering "in Christ." The various ways Paul describes believers (justified, belonging to Christ, having peace with God, reconciled to God, etc.) may be subsumed in what I take to be Paul's umbrella understanding of the significance of faith in Christ — through faith in Christ we participate in Christ's body and are one Spirit with Christ;[59] after we come to faith in Christ we become incorporated into Christ.[60] The shorthand for this is: we are "in Christ."[61]

Subsequent to faith in Christ all that we know and experience is known and experienced "in Christ." This, of course, includes the troubles of human life. "In Christ" suffering, then, refers to our experience of suffering as people who believe in Jesus Christ.

As believers we also experience suffering as a *result* of our being believers — what we might call believer-specific suffering. This suffering comes because we are suffering "with Christ."

A brief caveat: as other readers and admirers of Paul's dense, organic, and unsystematic thought in Romans will appreciate, I must remain less than certain that I have always correctly assigned Paul's thoughts to the "in Christ" and "with Christ" compartments I have constructed.

Another Context for Human Suffering: "in Christ"

The fact that believers are "in Christ" does not separate us from the fierceness of human travails, but it can provide a unique context for suffering.

59. So E. P. Sanders, *Paul and Palestinian Judaism: A Comparison of Patterns of Religion* (Philadelphia: Fortress, 1977), p. 463.

60. So J. A. Ziesler: "to believe is to be in Christ" (*The Meaning of Righteousness in Paul: A Linguistic and Theological Inquiry* [Cambridge: Cambridge University Press, 1972], p. 165).

61. A. Schweitzer, of course, long ago argued that Paul's soteriology can be seen to derive from the idea of "the eschatological doctrine of the being-in-Christ" (*The Mysticism of Paul the Apostle*, tr. W. Montgomery [London: Black, 1931], p. 220). See also A. Deissmann, *St. Paul: A Study in Social and Religious History*, tr. L. R. M. Strachan (London: Hodder and Stoughton, 1912), pp. 139-43.

Suffering "in Christ" Is Suffering in God's Life

Being "in Christ" means we have experienced a death: "our old self was crucified with [Christ]" (6:6).[62] The result of this death is that we are "no longer enslaved to sin" (6:6). Our liaison with sin has been severed, for we have been made righteous through faith, reconciled to God. Consequently, while sin clearly still strongly influences our existence as believers,[63] we need not be controlled by it.[64] We may even "consider [ourselves] dead to sin" (6:11). In a curious turn of phrase, Paul describes our "in Christ" situation as one in which we have been "justified from sin."[65] Whatever else this phrase means, it indicates separation from sin. Being "in Christ" is at the same time *not* being in the domain ruled by sin and death.[66] We are, in other words of Paul, not in the flesh but in the Spirit (8:9). We are at peace with God (5:1).

Through our death with Christ we receive a particular kind of life — life that separates us from death while also uniting us with death. The life we receive separates us from the kind of death that occurs in the lethal sin–death duo (5:12-14), while uniting us to the kind of death that Christ died (6:5) — a death which conclusively died to sin (6:10), thereby driving a permanent wedge between the potent partnership of

62. The idea of being crucified with Christ is distinct from the idea of suffering with Christ (8:17). In the former, Paul is referring to our *"transfer* to being a Christian" (Sanders, *Paul and Palestinian Judaism,* p. 463; see also p. 467 on Rom 6:3-11; I disagree with Sanders, however, in his connecting 8:17 with 6:3-11). As we shall see, Paul's reference to suffering "with Christ" (8:17) is to the ongoing requirement of suffering "which is inseparable from faithfulness to Christ in a world which does not yet know him as Lord" (Cranfield, *Romans,* I, p. 408). This is different from the idea here of our transfer into Christ through death with Christ.

63. In fact, much of Paul's epistolary energy is spent on addressing the continuing influence of sin among the converted.

64. T. J. Deidun writes: "For Paul, christian liberty is first and foremost radical emancipation from the power of sin and release from the impotence of self" (*New Covenant Morality in Paul* [Rome: Biblical Institute Press, 1981], p. 209).

65. 6:7; this is the translation Cranfield chooses for δεδικαίωται ἀπὸ τῆς ἁμαρτίας (*Romans,* I, p. 296).

66. Cf. L. E. Keck, "The Law and 'The Law of Sin and Death' (Rom 8:1-4): Reflections on the Spirit and Ethics in Paul," in *The Divine Helmsman,* pp. 41-58, here p. 53.

death and sin. [67] The life we receive "in Christ" unites us to Christ's death — a death that was not just a death to sin but also a death resulting in life (6:4).

Consequently, "in Christ" we suffer as people who know that our lot is not death but life (5:17-21; 6:1-11) and that this lot is both our hope and our present reality. We live now as those who are "alive from the dead,"[68] as those who have newness of life (6:4),[69] and so our suffering is transformed. Our suffering is, in K. Barth's remarkable words, "no longer a passive, dangerous, poisonous, destructive tribulation . . . but is transformed into a tribulation . . . which [is] creative, fruitful, powerful, promising."[70]

Furthermore, our belief that our bodies, like Christ's, will be resurrected, means that when we face physical death we can see beyond that terror to life. For we "in Christ" know that "he who raised Christ Jesus from the dead will give life to [our] mortal bodies" (8:11). The presence of God's Spirit in us assures us that even the death of our bodies cannot thwart God's loving desire to give and sustain life and only life. We therefore suffer in the face of a different kind of death from that which we suffered before and in which nonbelievers suffer now. Even though we will physically die, our death will not separate us from life. Our suffering takes place in the context of life.

We may then understand our inevitable troubles in a larger context than that of suffering alone. Our sufferings — signs of sin's ongoing activity — take place under the dome of God's life (6:11, 13), for God's life in-

---

67. Luther speaks of a twofold everlasting death: "the one is good and glorious; it is death unto sin, or the death of death, by which the soul is saved and separated from sin, as also the body is freed from corruption. By this death we are bound by grace and glory to the living God. . . . The other death is also everlasting, but absolutely destructive, for it is the death of the damned. Here man perishes while sin lives and remains forever and ever throughout eternity" (*Commentary on the Epistle to the Romans*, p. 101). Paul is sure that believers participate in the first sort of death — a death that brings us to life.

68. 6:13, Cranfield's translation.

69. Cranfield: "the newness of life of which Paul speaks here is a foretaste of the final renewal" (*Romans*, I, p. 305).

70. *Romans*, p. 156.

fuses our existence as those "in Christ." And so joy, patience, prayer, and the capacity to act in and for love may surround our tribulations (12:9-13).

Suffering "in Christ" Is Suffering in God's Love and Glory and in Hope

Being "in Christ" means that our hearts are filled with God's love for us, and so with our love for God.[71] Paul claims that the love of God has been poured into our hearts by means of the Holy Spirit (5:5). Having a love relationship with God provides for those "in Christ" a context completely different from the one we knew when we were enemies of God (5:10), handed over to our destructive desires (1:24). Consequently, the context in which believers experience suffering is shaped by God's loving presence.

Knowing God's love is at once to know God's glory. As K. Barth wrote, "the objective meaning of God's glory is His active grace and mercy and patience, His love."[72] And to know God's love is also to be able to hope to share in God's glory, for we know that God's love, which is God's glory, wishes to embrace God's creation (8:18). Paul is certain that the future for believers is one radiant with God's love in Christ Jesus our Lord (8:39), a radiance undisturbed by the shadows of sin. God's promise to believers is that "all will be well."[73] Our current pains are not the end of the story. As we suffer "in Christ," in the context of God's love, we are given the capacity to see the door that leads to God's glory and are enabled to wait for its opening.

Suffering "in Christ" produces hope (5:3-4).[74] We are enabled and

---

71. The genitive construction in 5:5 may be translated both ways and both should be understood here: "God's love" (the generally accepted reading, e.g., Cranfield, Dunn) will, through the Spirit, enable and energize our "love for God." As Stuhlmacher notes, the Holy Spirit allows us to "become capable of returning the love of God bestowed upon [us]" and so we "complete the state of grace into which [we] are transferred through the Christ" (*Romans*, p. 80).

72. Barth, *Church Dogmatics* II/1 (Edinburgh: Clark, 1957), p. 653.

73. Julian of Norwich's saying for the Christian hope.

74. This is a passage on which I am agnostic about whether its reference to suffer-

energized to see that there is something beyond suffering. Our sufferings are not a sign of our failure but are, strangely, a cause for our boasting (5:3).[75] We may fully embrace our human existence as it is, knowing that because we are "in Christ" there is a dynamism to it. We are on a trajectory to God's glory and so even our sufferings are active; they "produce endurance" (5:3). We can boast in them, we can even glory in them, for because we have been infused with God's love for us and our resultant love for God, we now see that "what at first seems nothing but mere human suffering [has] become the action of God, the Creator and Redeemer."[76] Our sufferings produce the necessary perseverance for a life of hope, a life that, in the midst of the current brokenness, can see God's love, believe in God's glory, and have faith that that glory will be shared with all that is. It is because we who are "in Christ" suffer in God's love that we can hope.[77]

The hope of the end of suffering, which is the same as the hope of sharing the glory of God, of being completely in the presence of the one who only heals and loves, exists together with the partial presence of that hope, for now we may suffer in God's love.

That our hope is partially realized is evident also in the fact that God has already shown God's love for humanity by giving up God's son for us (8:32) and did so for the purpose of salvation, of healing the source of suffering. God's love is, then, not only the love of presence but the presence of love.

God shows God's love for humanity by offering us righteousness — offering us God's own character (3:26; 5:8-9).[78] The revelation of God's

---

ing belongs to the "in Christ" or the "with Christ" category. Cranfield would, I think, agree with my choice here of assigning it to my "in Christ" category — the suffering shared with humanity but experienced "in Christ" (*Romans*, I, p. 261).

75. The word καυχάομαι is best translated not "rejoice," as it often is, but "boast" or "glory."

76. Barth, *Romans*, p. 156.

77. Cf. Barth: "By [love's] power, hope is not put to shame . . . even in tribulation" (*Romans*, p. 158).

78. The "righteousness of God" which results in our being justified (1:17; 3:21) can be understood as an appositive genitive ("righteousness, that is, God"). The righteous-

righteousness is the revelation of God's desire and power to save — to liberate all from sin and from death, to give all life (1:16-17). This revelation is the context in which believers in the good news suffer.

Of course, this revelation is more than a revelation of God's character, it is also an invitation to share in that character — perhaps the most amazing indication of God's love. Believers are people who are reconciled to God (5:10), who have peace with God (5:1), who are children of God (8:16). We are no longer God's enemies, but are now made righteous (5:1, 9). We have, in other words, "died to sin" (6:2). We are re-shaped so that we may now expect to share in the very glory of God (5:2). God's being is no longer foreign and inaccessible to us. We have been retooled, made righteous, made similar enough to God that we can expect eventually to bask fully in God's glory.

"In Christ" our suffering takes place in God's love, which is at once God's righteousness and glory.

"With Christ" Suffering

Paul is further convinced that believers take on sufferings in addition to those of the common lot of humanity. We suffer not only "in Christ" but also "with Christ." Suffering "with Christ" goes beyond our bringing our sufferings into Christ to our sharing Christ's sufferings[79] and our suffering for Christ's sake.[80]

Suffering "with Christ" is voluntary in the sense that it is only be-

---

ness of God revealed in the gospel is the nature of God, which is now available to those who believe in Jesus Christ. See L. A. Jervis, "Becoming like God through Christ: Discipleship in Romans," in *Patterns of Discipleship in the New Testament*, ed. R. N. Longenecker (Grand Rapids: Eerdmans, 1996), pp. 143-62, here pp. 155-59.

79. Fitzmyer reads "suffering with Christ" (8:17) in this way (*Romans*, p. 502). We see Paul saying this in different words in Phil 3:10, where he expresses his desire to know the fellowship of Christ's sufferings.

80. So Jewett, *Romans*, p. 503. Cranfield takes it that συμπάσχομεν (8:17) refers both to suffering for Christ's sake and in union with Christ and to the thought that "the exalted Christ participates in His brethren's sufferings" (*Romans*, I, p. 408).

cause a person believes in Jesus Christ that she takes on these additional sufferings: unlike the sufferings we share with humanity, these sufferings could be avoided. On the other hand, suffering "with Christ" is not an option once one is "in Christ." It is rather the normal state of things for those who are "in Christ."

Paul speaks directly of this aspect of believers' suffering in 8:17: "since indeed we suffer with [Christ] in order that we may be glorified with him." Paul's use of the word εἴπερ in this verse has generated diverse interpretations. Put simply, scholars are divided over whether Paul is admonishing believers to do something they are not yet doing — "provided that we suffer with [Christ]," or whether Paul is describing what is already occurring — "since indeed we suffer with [Christ]." There are several reasons that the second reading is best.[81]

Paul regards suffering "with Christ" as an unavoidable aspect of being "in Christ." Our conformity to Christ (8:29) requires ongoing suffering "with Christ."[82] It is to be noted, as mentioned above, that suffering "with Christ" is not the same as being baptized into Christ's death. The latter idea refers to our incorporation into Christ through faith. What we are talking about here is rather the inescapable activity of suffering with and for Christ that ensues upon our incorporation into Christ.

Paul hints at the concept that Christ's own sufferings continue in this time of incomplete salvation, and that they do so through believers. Paul (or a follower of his) says something similar in Col 1:24: "I complete what is lacking in Christ's afflictions."[83] These ongoing suffer-

---

81. Jewett, for instance, notes that 8:14-17 has an explanatory function, not an admonitory one. It is describing what is, not what should be (*Romans*, p. 502). This is confirmed by the fact that the verb συμπάσχομεν is in the present tense. Jewett, like others (e.g., Cranfield), translates εἴπερ in 8:17 as it is translated in 8:9, as descriptive of what is.

82. Cf. Cranfield, *Romans*, I, p. 432.

83. Col 1:24 goes on to say "for the sake of his body, that is, the church." In literary context, the source of the church is Christ and Christ is the one through "whom all things, whether on earth or in heaven" are reconciled (Col 1:18-20). In other words, here also is the thought that the suffering of believers is a share of Christ's redemptive sufferings.

ings of Christ embodied now in believers must be redemptive, just as were Christ's sufferings on the cross.[84] Our suffering "with Christ" is, like Christ's suffering, experienced on behalf of God's creation (human and non-human). The groaning of believers as the creation waits for our identity as God's children to be revealed (which revelation will mean creation's liberation, 8:19-23) is more than sharing the pain, more than groaning "with respect to ourselves."[85] It is groaning occasioned by an acute awareness that we are essential to the birthing of the age of liberation. It is, in other words, a groaning not only for ourselves but for all that is. In this we suffer "with Christ."

While believers, according to Paul, are required to suffer, we may do so in hope and with insight. However, the provision of hope and insight is not just sweet. It is also bitter, for, while our expectation and our perception allow us to suffer with a degree of peace and joy, they also are the cause of the peculiar tribulations we know.

Suffering "with Christ" in Hope: Future Hope

Suffering "with Christ" takes place within the horizon of hope for the end of sufferings. Paul claims that the sufferings we experience are not endless and permanent. There is something coming that is suffering's opposite: glory (8:17-18). This glory will be known by us and by all creation. As Käsemann says, Paul speaks of a hope that "reaches beyond believers to creation as a whole."[86] Paul opens a window onto the hope of participating in glory, which is to participate in God's be-

---

84. A. J. M. Wedderburn resists the idea that in Colossians the author is referring to Christ's passion on the basis simply of such an idea being theologically distasteful; "it mitigates . . . the possible implication that somehow Christ's sufferings had been deficient or insufficient" (*The Theology of the Later Pauline Letters* [Cambridge: Cambridge University Press, 1993], p. 38). He prefers to understand the meaning of Col 1:24 to be the "sufferings which now afflict those who now stand for him in this hostile world" (p. 39). What Wedderburn does not contemplate is that ongoing sufferings of Christ through Christ's body, the church, may have a redemptive significance.

85. Byrne's translation of 8:23 (*Romans*, p. 262). See Byrne, p. 264, for his solution to the riddle of the textual variants for this verse.

86. *Romans*, p. 234.

ing,[87] a reality from which sin is excluded.[88] Suffering is neither the only reality nor the only possibility; the reality of suffering and sin is juxtaposed with the reality of glory.

Paul raises believers' eyes to the hope of glory experienced completely, which is at once freedom from suffering, since it is complete separation from sin. The hope of believers — the hope of sharing in the glory of God (5:2) — is at the same time the hope of release from all travail.[89] While we suffer now, we do so with a certain confidence, for Christ's resurrection and glorification assures us of our own resurrection. We suffer knowing that we are now children of God, as Christ is God's son. As Christ inherited God's glory, so will we (8:16-17). Christ's death resulted in his glorification, in his being all that humanity was intended to be — beings basking in the glory of God.[90] This is the inheritance that waits for us.

Because of God's love, seen most clearly in Jesus Christ, whom God gave up for us all (8:32), we then suffer in hope, and so our suffering is limited by the certainty that we are being "conformed to the image of [God's] son" (8:29).[91] Just as Christ Jesus, the revealer of God's love (8:39), knew both suffering and glorification, so do we. We suffer knowing that the outcome of suffering is glory and so we will receive "all things with [Christ Jesus]" (8:32).

The Presence of Hope

The horizon of future hope, while at a distance, at the same time frames our current reality. The future hope shines into our present. The

87. Cf. Cranfield, who notes that the glory of God is God's self-manifestation (*Romans*, I, p. 120).

88. Sin and glory are mutually exclusive. To sin is to fall short of God's glory (3:23). Righteousness and glory are then of a piece.

89. When a person experiences glory to the full, that person also knows, in Cranfield's words, "the resurrection life of the blessed" (*Romans*, I, p. 147).

90. Cf. Dunn, *Romans*, p. 457.

91. Cf. Calvin: "all the afflictions of believers are simply the means by which they are conformed to Christ" (*Romans*, p. 180).

context of our sufferings is, then, both a future and a present hope. We suffer in hope of the end of suffering and the embrace of God's glory. We also suffer in the presence of that hope.[92]

Perhaps the clearest demonstration of the presence of hope is that the Spirit of God, which is to say, the Spirit of Christ,[93] lives in us (8:9). The Spirit's power may encourage us in hoping as a result of God, the giver of our hope, filling us with "all joy and peace in believing" (15:13).[94] The Spirit's presence is, in this sense, the presence of hope.

In the present time the Spirit is the presence of the future — of that time when God's will alone prevails. Believers, who are "weak" (8:26: presumably because of our former bondage to sin),[95] are recipients of the Spirit's intercessions on our behalf. These intercessions are, Paul says, according to God's will (8:27). That is, the presence of the Spirit is the presence of what we long for — complete accord with God's will — which will be the same as the end of suffering.

The Spirit is the "first fruits" (8:23), the guarantee that new life is on the horizon. Because we now have the Spirit we live in the presence of the hope that our identity as children of God will be realized.

This creates the tension intrinsic to our present hope: we suffer at sin's hands at the same time as we know the opposite experience — life,

92. Both Käsemann and Barth see this in Romans, although they disagree over how present the future is. Käsemann recognizes the apocalyptic aspect of Romans: that "the end time has already begun for Paul, his theme is not the relation of the aeons but the presence of life" (*Romans*, p. 142). Barth writes: "men do not pass beyond the threshold of the kingdom of God . . . yet they do stand hopefully on the threshold; and because they have hope, they do not wholly lack the anticipatorily present reality of what is hoped for" (*Romans*, p. 180).

93. Dunn rightly recognizes that here Paul is defining the Spirit of God as the Spirit of Christ (*Romans*, p. 429).

94. Translating "God of hope" as a genitive of source (so, Cranfield, *Romans*, II, p. 747).

95. Calvin understands this reference to "weakness" to be to the challenges of "bearing the cross [which] is beyond their own strength" (*Romans*, p. 311). Barth understands Paul's reference to weakness as a reference to our creatureliness (*Romans*, p. 316). However, in view of the fact that a few sentences earlier Paul spoke of "the flesh" (in this case, a coordinate of sin) as weakening the law (8:3), Paul may be alluding here to *our* having been weakened by sin; cf. my interpretation of 7:14.

which is the result of righteousness (8:10). While this tension produces hope, it may also add to our suffering. We who have the "first fruits" of the age of liberation are stretched between that time and this. We are pulled between our firm knowledge (given to us by the Spirit) that there will be an end to pain — the redemption of our bodies,[96] and our acute awareness and experience of the sufferings of this present time.

Suffering "with Christ" with Insight

We Suffer Because We See.   Paul works to give believers insight into our sufferings. This insight does not take away our pain. Paul's view is, rather, that we suffer in part because we know too much. For instance, Paul can see the predicament of his fellow Jews and exposes for others to see his wrenching anguish over their unbelief (9:1-3). He further helps believers recognize the source of some of our anguish. We are, Paul says, excruciatingly aware of the pain of creation, for we are the ones who know (8:22) the travail creation is in.

Our suffering is partially due to the fact that we cannot hide from the pain that is. Our very sight is our suffering. We see that creation is in bondage to corruption, that decay hangs over everything (8:21).

Moreover, we know that now is the time of waiting for salvation (5:9-10),[97] of waiting for our resurrection and our glorification, and so it is the time of our suffering. The drama of Christ's life is the drama of our own, and we know that we are in the period before resurrection and so will suffer. We know that our present context is one of suffering with Christ (8:17) and *hoping* to share in glory with Christ; we hope for glory and, while we hope, we suffer.

Paul opens his hearers' eyes to the reality that there is a shape to

96. Cf. Käsemann's comment on 8:23: "for Paul the resurrection of the dead was no mere symbol of openness to the future but the end of earthly pain" (*Romans*, p. 238).

97. The future of σώζω in these verses indicates that salvation as a "share in the risen life of Christ" is still something we await (so, Fitzmyer, *Romans*, p. 401). Dunn speaks of this time as the "period between reconciliation and salvation" (*Romans*, p. 261).

our sufferings: they are shaped by our call to be conformed to Christ (8:28-29). By virtue of being caught between the time of Christ's resurrection and the time of our own we recognize that we will suffer as we hope for glory.

We Suffer Because We Can Resist. Our suffering "with Christ" is caused not by our enslavement to sin but by sin's pressing its deteriorating but still powerful muscle against the bruises left from our prior indenture. Like the post-colonial country that is no longer required to take its identity from the colonizer or obey the colonizer's wishes but which nevertheless finds it exceedingly challenging to live out of an identity of freedom, so Paul recognizes that believers, while freed from sin, are still profoundly shaped by our previous servitude to it.[98]

We are nevertheless strong enough to choose to resist sin's force, and so we will know struggle. Although we are not fully healed or fully free of sin's devastating force, we are empowered to count ourselves "dead to sin and alive to God in Christ Jesus" (6:11; cf. 6:7). As we have seen, this context allows us to see our inevitable sharing in humanity's suffering in the context of God's life and love, but, as we shall see, it also produces an inevitable increase in our sufferings. We are liberated from sin in order to struggle against it.[99]

Believers have insight into the reality that there is a battle going on between God and sin and that, even though the outcome of the battle is known, the time for that outcome is not yet. We suffer difficulties (8:35), but these manifestations of sin's muscle need not terrify us,[100] for believers know that these sufferings will not separate us from Christ's love and that we are promised all that Christ has now received

98. See L. A. Jervis, "Reading Romans 7 in Conversation with Post-Colonial Theory," *Theoforum* 35 (2004): 173-94.

99. Cf., Käsemann: "The old aeon, rebellious, threatening and perverted, is still present, so that Christians are under attack" (*Romans*, p. 247).

100. Byrne notes that there are two lists in this passage: 8:35b and 8:38-39a. The first details earthly difficulties and the second heavenly opponents. He argues that "the logic of the passage" suggests that "the physical trials listed in 35b are . . . the manifestation of the hostility of (the) super-human forces listed later on" (*Romans*, p. 277).

(8:35, 32).[101] Nevertheless, we recognize that we are now in the line of sin's fire and so must "put on the armor of light" (13:12), which is to say "the Lord Jesus Christ" (13:14).[102] Believers know that we have to fight against sin and maintain vigilance as we claim our place in the context of God's peace and life and freedom and righteousness.

Paul commands believers not to let sin reign in our bodies (6:12) nor to let them be used in sin's service (6:13). We are commanded to put ourselves at God's service (6:13). We are part of a battle for justice, for the existence of righteousness in this world. P. Stuhlmacher writes: "Christians should . . . place themselves at the disposal of God to be vanguards of the righteousness which corresponds to God's will."[103] The high stakes and the challenge of this battle are emphasized by Paul.

To serve God is to be assured of becoming holy as God is holy and of sharing in the divine life (6:22-23). That Paul strains to encourage believers to act as slaves of righteousness, slaves of God, indicates how challenging it is to do so. Clearly, believers can be drawn to the familiar patterns of sin, even though we know that that is a dead end. Paul labors to clear our vision of the bright lights of sin so that we can see the real landscape of reality: there is a battle taking place between sin and God, and God requires that believers stand with God. As Käsemann says, "baptism means that we become Christian soldiers in the corporeal sphere and in daily life in the world."[104] Paul's appeal that his hearers present their bodies as a living sacrifice (12:1) recognizes that living for God requires "giving of one's body and life in the service of righteousness."[105]

---

101. Fitzmyer notes that τὰ πάντα here is open-ended and so "must refer to everything pertaining to eschatological salvation" (*Romans*, p. 532). Stuhlmacher rightly relates this verse to Paul's idea in 8:17 of our fully participating in our promised inheritance along with Christ (*Romans*, p. 139).

102. Stuhlmacher comments: "Christians are still engaged — like their Lord himself — in the battle against the power and influences of darkness" (*Romans*, p. 213).

103. *Romans*, p. 93. See also Byrne, *Romans*, p. 194.

104. *Romans*, p. 363.

105. Stuhlmacher, *Romans*, p. 188, commenting on 12:1. Cf. W. T. Wilson, *Love without Pretense" Romans 12.9-21 and Hellenistic-Jewish Wisdom Literature* (Tübingen: Mohr, 1991), pp. 129-30.

This struggle exists not only outside ourselves, that is, between God and sin, with our serving on God's side, the side of righteousness (6:18). The struggle also takes place within ourselves. In the depths of our being there is a battle going on that mirrors the battle for justice that is taking place throughout creation. This battle inevitably contributes to our suffering.

Paul describes this struggle in Romans 7. While the current scholarly consensus is that the person describing the challenge posed by sin in Rom 7:7-25 is one who is not "in Christ,"[106] I have argued that Paul is here depicting the battle that takes place within the believer.[107] This, of course, is the classic view going back to such as Luther and the mature Augustine. Here we will proceed without argument on the basis of the understanding that Paul is speaking here of a struggle germane to the believer. (Whether or not Paul's first person singular refers to himself or to a representative believer is tangential to our current enterprise.)

At 7:8b Paul turns his attention to life in the new sphere "apart from law" — a sphere that did not exist until the manifestation of God's righteousness "apart from law."[108] This is a different reality from the reality that existed *before* the law. In this new reality sin is dead, and this for two reasons. First, because this reality "apart from law" is the reality of the revelation of God's righteousness (3:21), from which sin is excluded, and secondly because sin has lost its most effective instrument: it is the law that counts and increases sin (5:13, 20).

Paul recalls how he (or a representative person) once found himself in the blissful place apart from law (7:9a). The speaker here remembers the position of knowing himself freed from sin, of being apart from law and so of being alive. We may legitimately, albeit speculatively, pro-

---

106. The modern work typically credited with making this case most strongly is that of P. Meyer, "The Worm at the Core of the Apple: Exegetical Reflections on Romans 7," in *The Conversation Continues: Studies in Paul and John in Honor of J. L. Martyn*, ed. R. T. Fortna and B. R. Gaventa (Nashville: Abingdon, 1990), pp. 62-84.

107. L. A. Jervis, "'The Commandment Which Is for Life' (Romans 7.10): Sin's Use of the Obedience of Faith," *Journal for the Study of the New Testament* 27 (2004): 193-216.

108. I refer the reader to my article for the arguments behind this and subsequent interpretations of Rom 7:7-25 here presented.

pose that Paul's conviction that those "in Christ" are dead to sin and alive to God and should reckon themselves so (6:1-11) is rooted in this experience. While this experience was only temporary, it may have formed Paul's understanding of the basis and possibilities of life "in Christ." Barth's comment on 7:12-13 is that it expresses "the longing for the recovery of the lost immediacy of my life in God."[109]

This trajectory of freedom was, however, impeded when the "commandment" came (7:9b). This commandment, which in 7:10 Paul describes as a commandment meant to lead to life (and so, as I argue, it cannot be a commandment of Torah),[110] is the requirement to live in the "obedience of faith."[111] After reckoning with his liberation, Paul comes to see (and he wants others to share his insight) that the freedom God grants "apart from law" and "in Christ" is freedom to serve God's righteousness (cf. 6:18, 22), and this means struggle.

Servitude to God is at once conflict with sin. For while sin may be mortally wounded in this time of the revelation of God's righteousness and wrath (1:16-18), its pernicious presence has not been obliterated. It still has enough strength to revive (7:9b) and afflict the believer. In fact, the believer is particularly attuned to sin's ways. Believers can actually *see* (7:23) the battle with sin taking place within ourselves. As Cranfield writes: "in the Christian believer . . . (there) is a growing knowledge and . . . deepening hatred of sin."[112] We are aware that sin lives in us.

Unfortunately, insight into the conflict with sin that believers undergo does not lessen the fierceness of that battle. By serving God, the righteous one, we are necessarily the enemies of sin. We become, then, particularly important targets of sin. The fact that we are now sin's enemies is complicated by the fact that we once belonged to sin. Having been once sin's slaves (7:14) means that, even though we know we are no longer required to serve sin, our tendencies, shaped by our former

109. *Romans*, p. 256.

110. It is to be noted that the concept of life is only connected with Christ for Paul. See Jervis, "'The Commandment Which Is for Life,'" p. 205.

111. I argue that ἐντολή in 7:9-13 has a different referent than it does in 7:8. In 7:9-13 it refers to the commandment inherent to faith in Christ.

112. *Romans*, I, p. 359.

captivity, draw us toward doing that very thing.[113] Having once been the property of sin means that in effect sin still lives in us, even while we may be dead to it.

Paul is realistic, perhaps because of his personal and pastoral experience, about the abiding influence of sin in the life of faith. In fact, the life of faith may be a life in which sin's influence is most clearly seen. The commandment which leads to life (7:10), that is, the obedience of faith, challenges sin such that sin revives itself for the purpose of attempting to re-enslave the one who seeks to obey God's righteousness. For complete obedience to the commandment of God is lethal for sin. Such obedience, as Christ's own perfect obedience demonstrates, renders sin dead.

The anguish Paul expresses in 7:7-25 is that of the believer struggling continually against sin. This is an experience of suffering peculiar to believers who have insight into the nature of the task to which God has called us. We are on the side of justice, of righteousness, and are called to and capable of resisting sin's proliferation of suffering. (Though the speaker in Romans 7 says he fails to resist sin, he is anything but apathetic. The drama of this discourse comes from his attempt at resistance.) This challenge is, however, not uncomplicated, for our former indenture to sin still shapes us.

We Can See God's Love as We Suffer. Paul does not let believers forget that the battle that rages within and without ourselves is circumscribed by God's love, which is at once Christ's love (8:35, 37, 39). Divine love defines for believers the limits and the outcome of the battle. The battle against sin is framed by the fact that God's love is revealed in Christ Jesus our Lord (8:39). Jesus, whom, as God's Son, was handed over for all of us (8:32), epitomizes love — a love that shares our pain in order to take away our pain. Sin's power, in other words, was decisively limited at the cross.

---

113. Reading πεπραμένος ὑπὸ τὴν ἁμαρτίαν in context as referring to a past occurrence which affects the present. The speaker is no longer bound to that past (he is capable of recognizing the spiritual), although he is influenced by it.

This means that, as we stand against sin, we can know ourselves to be "more than conquerors" (8:37) even as we know ostensible defeats (8:35) and ongoing struggle (7:9-24). For we are enabled by divine love (8:37)[114] to recognize and resist: to recognize that sin's power, manifested in suffering, is in fact weaker than love — the cross and resurrection is proof of this; and so we may resist the temptation to dumbly succumb to sin's terrors — we may instead trust God.[115]

Summary

Sin is the source of suffering. When humans suffer, even from disease or natural calamities, the cause of that suffering is sin. (This is not to be misunderstood as warrant for blaming an individual's suffering on his or her particular sins.) Paul's concern with sin is at once his concern for humanity's afflictions. It is because of sin's presence that suffering is a fact of our existence. This presence is envisioned by Paul as both a force capable of bending humanity to its will and a presence in the very being of humankind. Sin's presence both co-opts us and finds an ally in us.

Paul both joins and separates believers and nonbelievers in regard to their suffering as a result of sin's malicious presence. According to Paul, all humanity, whether of the saved or not-saved variety, groan in this time of waiting for the ultimate defeat of sin, that is, the end of suffering. Paul recognizes sin's power to produce sufferings in every human life, whether or not one believes in Jesus Christ. All humankind shares the same history — a history of bondage to sin. All humankind shares a common future, at least in the short term — our bodies die as a result of the lethal sin-death partnership which at present structures our reality. Furthermore, believers and nonbelievers

114. The referent of "through him who loved us" in 8:37 is to Christ and Christ's enacting God's love for us at the cross (5:8-10).

115. Cf. Käsemann: "precisely afflicted faith trusts in the love of Christ against all appearances" (*Romans*, p. 254).

are joined in the suffering of lack of trust in God's righteousness, with its resultant existential angst and pointless attempts to conceive of and create justice apart from the justice of God. This state of resistance to God, which is suspicious of God's trustworthiness and goodness, means that we all live in a state of uncertainty and bear the weight of fear and of pride.

Despite the commonalities of human suffering, Paul does differentiate between those who believe in Christ and those who do not in regard to sufferings. Nonbelievers are, in Paul's view, mastered by sin such that they have no option but to both suffer and generate afflictions. According to Paul, only from the position of being "in Christ" may sin be resisted. Paul even judges his fellow Jews to be cooperators with sin and so proliferators of suffering. All those who are apart from Christ are, for Paul, positioned under the dark cloud of death and of God's coming wrath.

Believers, on the other hand, have an alternative context for suffering and an added experience of it. Paul distinguishes believers' suffering from that of nonbelievers in two ways. First, while the converted and the unconverted may live in a world in which sin is present, believers may experience the resultant sufferings in a unique context — the context of being "in Christ." Secondly, those who have faith in Jesus Christ also take on sufferings "with Christ."

For people who believe in Christ, the common lot of human suffering may be undergone "in Christ." This allows believing sufferers to bear their afflictions in the light of God's life and love, and in the certainty of a future freed from sin's claws. The converted suffer in the arena of hope for suffering's end, surrounded in the suffering moment by God's embracing love. In fact, believers' sufferings may even open our eyes to the presence of God's love and to the glory (i.e., absence of sin and suffering) that is our future. Life and not death, salvation and not suffering, may encircle our experience of the troubles of human life.

In the context of being "in Christ" believers do not only experience, albeit in a different way, what they would have experienced anyway. Being "in Christ" requires also that believers suffer "with Christ." Believers take on extra sufferings by virtue of being believers: they are required to suffer "with Christ." This suffering allows our conformity to Christ and is on behalf of God's creation (human and non-human). This extra burden is lightened somewhat by the provision of hope and of insight. The hope entailed in suffering "with Christ" is the hope that we, like Christ, will be glorified and receive all things with Jesus. This hope for a future reward for our sufferings "with Christ" is also present to a degree. Even now, as we suffer "with Christ" we are being changed into his glorious likeness. Especially as we embrace the presence of the Spirit and allow our petitions to be shaped by the Spirit, we become even now what we will become — people who like Jesus Christ live in full accord with God's will, a will which does not include suffering. In the present, suffering "with Christ" is at the same time a striving to defeat suffering.

Sufferers "with Christ" also have insight into our sufferings. We are aware of creation's groaning for liberation from decay. This awareness increases our suffering. We are aware of the moment in which we are caught — the moment before we share in Christ's glory. We may also perceive our freedom to resist sin's power and our responsibility to struggle against it. We recognize that we are part of a battle for God's justice and that this battle is taking place both outside ourselves and within us. We perceive that we are now sin's enemies by virtue of being God's servants and that our former slavery to sin complicates our attempt at service to God. We may also have insight into the reality of love that surrounds us as we suffer "with Christ," which is the same as understanding that despite sin's (i.e., suffering's) bite and power, God's good will for creation will prevail.

Using Romans to Talk about Suffering

Romans offers important insights into our experience of suffering; insights that have the potential to pierce our beings so that we may know in the entirety of ourselves and in the living of our lives the transforming reality of Paul's words.

Suffering Is an Affront to Human Dignity

Romans may in the first instance be used to confirm that the difficulties of human life are real. Paul's view on suffering here is unblinkered. And he does not promote (either for believers or nonbelievers) anything less than our outrage at pain, loss, mental anguish, and death.

Suffering for Paul is the result of God's enemy — sin. The opposite of suffering is God's righteousness and glory, in which there is no sin and consequently only peace and joy and life and love. While now God's glory includes God's participation with us in the experience of suffering — the most dramatic manifestation of this being God's gift to us of God's Son (3:21-26) — the glory of God exists perfectly (and will ultimately be all there is) *at the same time* as God involves Godself with sin.

The Unity of Humanity

Paul balances his stress on believers' liberation from a past of being oppressed by sin with his calling our attention to the presence of this past in our current existence. Even though we are "in Christ," we still share, we still continue to share, the same history as unbelievers. Believers are not separated from the rest of humanity through our conversion to Christ. Quite the opposite — in the light of God's glory the unity of humanity is made visible. We all, even those who are "in" God's Christ, are drawn to God's enemy — sin.

Paul charges that all humanity has a common history, summed up most graphically in the sordid list of sufferings at the end of the first chapter of Romans. Paul, of course, thinks that the therapy for the world's ills has been provided in Christ and that believers can now participate in God's healing project. Nevertheless, it is important to notice that Paul does not let us believers forget our roots. We share with nonbelievers a history of slavery of such a virulent sort that that shameful history is capable of almost unstoppable reproduction. Slavery to sin, with its resultant suffering and death, is the past that believers share with those who have not turned to Jesus Christ. Regrettably, for nonbelievers that past is also their present, and, for believers, that past still invades our present.

The dark visage of physical death sneering behind the radiant foreground of the gospel Paul preaches in Romans indicates his recognition that humanity is imprisoned in the inescapability of death. Paul features death starkly in his portrait of life apart from Christ, and, even while painting the landscape of life "in Christ," Paul draws the eye to death's presence.

The starting point for understanding our suffering as believers is, then, that it is *human* suffering. We are one with all humans who share life on this sin-battered planet. This recognition about who we are may shape our attitudes both to ourselves and to those who do not share our faith.

Paul's Concern for Those Not "in Christ"

The concern Paul has for those who are not "in Christ" is that they are unaware of the new reality in which the seemingly iron-clad dominance of sin, and so of suffering, was broken through Christ's death and resurrection. Consequently, for Paul, unbelievers are unable to enjoy and enable suffering's opposite — righteousness/justice, peace with God, life, and the embrace of God's love and glory.

In Paul's view, the unconverted are sin's pawns, which means at once that they allow sin to have its way in the world and have profound suffering of their own. Speaking from the perspective of one who knows that life has defeated death, Paul's concern for those who are not "in Christ" is that they live without the knowledge that death has been conquered by life. In Paul's view, they live without hope; they live in fear.[116] Moreover, unless they accept God's offer of becoming, through Christ, sin's opposite (i.e., righteous), they contribute to suffering's longevity. As Paul explicates in Romans 1, behavior that results from not acknowledging God or living in gratitude to God (1:21), that is, behavior

116. In 8:15 Paul speaks about the fear that believers have been liberated from.

that is ungodly and unrighteous, hurts others, destroys trust and so community, and does not allow for peace and wisdom. Such behavior, rooted in sin, causes suffering.

From the vantage point of one who knows the liberty of being embraced by God's love in Christ, those apart from Christ Jesus live under the law of sin and death (8:2). That is, according to Paul, nonbelievers live thinking that humanity's troubles and the sad fate of every person to die are unavoidable. They live now as slaves of the very thing that harms them most — sin. This terrifying bondage Paul describes as "living in the flesh" — a condition in which the passions of sin may not be checked, even by the law, and consequently these passions flourish and become fodder for death (7:5). Implicit in Paul's focus on sin's pernicious power is his recognition of the immense capacity that experiences of suffering has to limit our trust in God and our gratitude for life itself.

Paul's warning that humanity's wickedness deserves God's wrath (2:5) is at the same time his expression of deep and concerned interest in humanity's suffering. It is a warning meant to encourage recognition that trading in sin, which feeds suffering like cancer cells feed a tumor, actually has no future. Nonbelievers are, in Paul's view, riding a destructive, dead-end train, and he does not derive any smug satisfaction from this.

Making Paul's Concern Our Own

We may choose to adopt Paul's concern as our own — our interest in those who do not share our faith may become primarily a concern about their being caught in a devastating cycle of suffering. If we wish to take Paul as our example, our attitude toward non-Christians would be profound love and compassion, care for the present and future lives of all of humanity, outrage when tribulations occur to any person or part of this planet. Our attitude and actions toward those outside our faith, in other words, would be motivated only by concern for their well-being.

Suffering "in Christ"

At the same time as Paul's words may be used to emphasize the connectedness of humanity and indeed of all that is, they also help those who believe in Christ to see our sufferings in a distinctive light. Paul thinks that believers in Christ now inhabit a reality which, though sharing in the commonalities of human existence, at the same time provides a particular filter. In Paul's view, the converted, while not translated out of this world of sorrows, are not required to be shaped by it. Believers are "in Christ" and so our experience of the troubles of human life may be shaped by the distinctive environment offered "in Christ." Rather than sufferings separating the sufferer from God or from a sense of the presence of love or the energy of hope, those "in Christ" may know God's life even as we experience pain and face or go through death. "In Christ" we may understand that the sufferings (whatever they may be) that we, like all other humans must endure, are bounded by life.

As those "in Christ" we may know that the horizons of the place in which we experience suffering are the horizons of God's loving presence. We may know ourselves to be suffering in the context of love, of knowing that God loves us and of being able to love God despite our suffering. Believers in Christ may recognize that God's love more than shares our pain: it seeks to take away our pain so that only love will be present. We may know that the love of God is such that not only does it surround us as we bear suffering's sting, but it will also eventually bring us to a place without pain (8:31-39).

"In Christ" the burdens of human life take place within the contours of God's love, which is at once God's glory and God's righteousness. Our trials may become material which God, in God's love, uses to reveal God's presence and the radiant life with which God longs to embrace us.[117]

Believers still know the influence of sin. Believers feel the effects of the sins of others and of the decay and corruption of creation (often, as

---

117. Cf. Gieniusz, *Romans 8:18-30*, p. 282.

suggested above, experienced as disease or natural disaster, and certainly experienced as physical death). And we may be aware of the inner struggle to rid ourselves of the destructive draw of sin, which leads us to harm others, ourselves, and God's creation and furthermore robs us of the equanimity that only comes from complete trust in God.[118]

As we have seen, however, Paul's perspective is that our suffering "in Christ" may be enveloped by constructive energies which are ultimately stronger than the fiercest tribulations. Our distrust of God, with its resultant anxieties (9:14) and shaky self-aggrandizement (11:25), may be eclipsed by trusting acceptance of our finitude and adoration of God's freedom and divinity and glory (11:33-36), by our faith in God's love. Our experience of the terrifying entropy of creation may be bounded by our conviction that God's life neither ends nor will ultimately be limited by creation's current state of decay.

The context of our suffering as those "in Christ" allows us to see that God's wrath is on the horizon, and, as it draws near, so does the certainty that God will finally and decisively obliterate sin from God's creation.[119] And we who are baptized, who have participated in Christ's death and so are made like Christ the righteous one (6:3; 5:9), can be assured that when that wrath comes conclusively, we will not be exposed to its cleansing power. Believers have the hope that, while our afflictions have a present tense, they do not have a future.

This means we can even say that all our sufferings work together for good.[120] It is life and not death, salvation and not suffering, that surrounds our experience of the trials of life. For we may experience our

---

118. As we saw above, trust in God is the only means of sidelining sin.

119. Paul says that God's wrath is being revealed (1:18) and that it will be revealed on the "day of wrath" (2:5). The present and the future aspects of wrath accord, of course, with the present and the future aspects of God's righteousness. God's righteousness (the flipside of God's wrath) is now revealed in the gospel, but the full revelation of God's righteousness awaits the day that is "at hand" (13:12). Likewise, God's wrath is now present in the gospel and its proclamation (so Cranfield, *Romans*, I, p. 109), but not yet in its fullness (so Fitzmyer, *Romans*, p. 108).

120. Rom 8:28. πάντα in 8:28 refers back to the suffering in 8:18 (see Käsemann, *Romans*, p. 244).

human suffering "in Christ," the righteous one, whose death ended in life and whose suffering inaugurated the end of suffering.

We "in Christ" remain fully human and so we are affected by sin's infection of creation. Nevertheless, according to Paul, we may experience and interpret and respond to our inevitable sufferings by claiming our place "in Christ." From the vantage point of this "in Christ" place, sufferings may be regarded as bounded by life and love and hope. It is possible from this perspective even to know peace and joy at the same time as we suffer. Again, this is not the same as denying the reality and the sting of suffering. Peace and joy do not cancel out suffering but may rather be suffering's companions.

More than the wonder of being offered such a context in which to experience the trials of human life — the "in Christ" context — Paul believes that the gospel requires its recipients to reach out from this place. We not only suffer with humanity but "with Christ" for humanity. Believers are provided both a unique environment in which human suffering may be undergone and a unique imperative to take on additional sufferings on account of ourselves and on account of God and God's creation — human and non-human.

Suffering "with Christ": What It Means for Us, for God, and for God's Creation

For Us

Suffering "with Christ" assures us of our future release from suffering — our glorification (8:17). Suffering "with Christ," suffering because we are in the first instance believing human beings, rather than because we are humans who believe, is in some senses purely pragmatic: unless we suffer "with Christ" we may not expect glory (8:17). Suffering "with Christ" is the *unbidden,* unavoidable, and necessary stage that we, like Christ, must pass through in order to obtain what Christ has obtained already.

Paul opens our eyes to the reality that our suffering "with Christ" is shaped by Christ. We suffer "with Christ" and so we suffer with the one whose sufferings ended suffering. Our sufferings are not ours alone, indicative of our alienation from God and our exile under sin's bondage. Rather, our sufferings are shared with Christ, the one who defeats sin, and so the hope of our future glory is being realized (8:17). In fact, now there is a "hidden glorification" taking place for believers.[121]

Suffering "with Christ" serves not only our future but also our present. It conforms us to Christ who is both the suffering one and the glorified one. For while we must primarily wait and hope to be conformed to Christ's glory, by suffering along with the one who alone is not dominated by sin's power we, along with him, overcome sin. In the freedom to overcome sin, which we know only by being in God's Christ (7:24–8:1), and which necessitates suffering "with Christ" (8:17), we already taste something of the glory that awaits us. For God's glory destroys and disdains sin. In the life of God, in the glory of God, there is no sin, and sin has no influence on God's glory. By suffering "with Christ," which is to suffer with the one over whom sin has no influence and by whom sin was mortally wounded, we already know something of God's glory. In this time of suffering we, by suffering "with Christ," are touched by the life that has finally healed all sufferings.

We cannot understand Paul's thought on this if we think only linearly. Paul says more than that we are now in a time of suffering "with Christ," waiting and hoping for the coming time of glory. He says also that at the same time as we suffer "with Christ" we also share Christ's life beyond suffering — we are now "glorified" (8:30).[122] The reality of suffering "with Christ" and the reality of eternal life are not only sequential but also simultaneous. This is so because "to God there is neither 'before nor after.'"[123]

Suffering "with Christ," then, positively affects at once our future

---

121. Byrne (*Romans*, p. 270), who takes seriously the aorist ἐδόξασεν in 8:30. Barth, who is cautious about the presence of the future, will nevertheless speak of a "creaturely *glorificatio*" that "takes place this side of redemption" (*Church Dogmatics* II/1, p. 669).

and our present. This experience of the presence of the future is, however, also our burden. For while the hope of glory may invigorate us it will also make us sober, starkly aware that we do not yet possess this glorious future. To live in this hope while suffering "with Christ" is both the source of joy and a special burden.[124] It is in part the "suffering of frustration" which is a "specifically Christian suffering. . . . Such suffering has what is hoped for as its cause."[125]

The only way to bear the weight of waiting while suffering "with Christ" is, as Paul says, with patience (8:25).[126]

For God and God's Creation

Beyond being of import to believers themselves, suffering "with Christ" is of value to God. God longs to include all creation in God's glory and does this through the death of Christ Jesus and our faith in that gift (3:23-25a). The welcome Christ provides for us (15:7) on the basis of his sacrificial suffering (15:3)[127] serves the glory of God (15:7).[128] Just as God

---

122. As just mentioned, the aorist ἐδόξασεν refers to, in Byrne's words, a "hidden glorification." Sanday and Headlam understand the verb to be "attracted" to the aorist tense and to indicate that "though not complete in its historical working out, the step implied in ἐδόξασεν is both complete and certain in the Divine counsels" (*Romans*, p. 218).

123. Sanday and Headlam, *Romans*, p. 218.

124. Cf. J. M. Scott: "the reason why believers groan in themselves as they eagerly await the resurrection — redemption of their mortal bodies is *because* they have the 'first fruits' of the indwelling Spirit" (*Adoption as Sons of God: An Exegetical Investigation into the Background of YIOΘΕΣΙΑ in the Pauline Corpus* [Tübingen: Mohr, 1992], p. 257).

125. Gieniusz, *Romans 8:18-30*, pp. 207-9.

126. Calvin notes the burden of lacking the good we know is there for us and recognizes in this reference to "patience" the only means for our waiting not to mean that the promise vanishes away (*Romans and Thessalonians*, p. 176).

127. Fitzmyer rightly understands this verse to refer to Christ's giving of his life, motivated by his love for humanity (*Romans*, p. 702).

128. 15:7 can be read as Paul saying that Christ accepted believers for the sake of God's glory or as Paul encouraging his hearers to do what he has asked them to do, to the glory of God. I agree with Käsemann (*Romans*, p. 384) and others (e.g., Dunn, *Romans*, p. 846) in choosing the first reading.

is served by Christ's suffering for and with us, so God's glory is served by *our* suffering "with Christ."

God's glory is at once God's complete freedom from sin and God's desire to free humanity from sin's tentacles. Christ's suffering serves God's glory because, for reasons beyond human understanding or logic, it gives humanity the wherewithal to escape sin's grasp and be embraced by the glory of God. When we suffer "with Christ" we suffer with the one who overcomes sin. We suffer, in other words, for God's glory.

God's glory is served by our suffering "with Christ" not only because we are fulfilling God's desire for us ourselves to reflect God's glory instead of being overshadowed by the destructiveness of sin, but also because we are helping to expand the arena in which God's glory may be witnessed. The goal of God's glory as it relates to God's creation is freedom for all to experience life untainted by decay (8:21). In Paul's terms this means, of course, life untouched by sin, since sin and death (decay) are codependents.[129] By suffering "with Christ," which is to participate in overcoming sin and so be embraced by God's glory, believers work along with God and Christ in defeating sin and increasing the room for God's glory.

Suffering "with Christ" aids the purpose of God's glory — life and only life for all that is. Our suffering as believers is necessary for the expansion of God's glory, just as was Christ's suffering.

On the ground, this will take the form of working for and with God's justice. For, as we noted above, God's righteousness/justice[130] and God's glory are for Paul equivalent concepts. Enacting God's justice, which is the same thing as reflecting and being embraced by God's glory, means for us suffering, just as it did for Christ.

Moreover, since, as God shows in giving Christ for the whole world (8:32), God longs for God's justice to be known by all, those who believe

---

129. We saw above that φθορά in 8:21 is the opposite of incorruptibility — it is the state that leads not to life but to death.

130. Of course the Greek word δικαιοσύνη in the phrase δικαιοσύνη θεοῦ means both "justice" and "righteousness."

in the revelation of God's justice in Christ (1:16-17) are necessarily called to serve that righteousness (6:18) in every circumstance.[131] This requires promoting God's righteousness where humans are still blinded to it. Our suffering "with Christ" is important, then, for all of God's creation, for as we suffer for God's righteousness, as we suffer "with Christ," our fellow humans may be offered, even provided, an escape from the downward spiral of sin, that is, suffering.

Our suffering "with Christ" may break the chains that imprison individual people and social networks and organizations and cultures in self-defeating and other-destroying ways of life. To suffer "with Christ" is to work for justice and life in our daily situations. Suffering "with Christ" is the same as allowing the love of God which has been poured into our hearts (5:5) to plunge us into places thirsty for God's love; it is to "overcome evil with good" (12:21). Käsemann's words reinforce my thoughts here: believers "must occupy the place on earth which [Christ] has left; . . . by allowing Christians to suffer with Christ, the Spirit brings about the transforming of the old creation."[132]

Paul does not prescribe what suffering "with Christ" should look like for his hearers. Although he refers to "tribulation, distress, persecution, famine, nakedness, peril, and sword" (8:35), these appear to be by and large his own experiences of suffering "with Christ"[133] and not a legislated list of such. This silence is expressive of Paul's certainty that "with Christ" sufferings will come unbidden. They will be shaped by the (all too numerous) situations in which Christ's suffering presence — through believers — must be offered.

Believers in Jesus Christ are exhorted by Paul's words in Romans to see and accept our obligation to share in God's care for God's creation — human and non-human. As sin, and so suffering, remain at work in

131. Others rightly connect our being made righteous through faith in Christ with our ability to do God's justice here and now. See, e.g., Tamez, *Amnesty of Grace*, p. 127; Byrne, *Romans*, p. 194; W. Altmann, *Luther and Liberation: A Latin American Perspective*, tr. M. Solberg (Minneapolis: Fortress, 1992), p. 39.

132. *Romans*, p. 234.

133. Commentators regularly note that all except the last are sufferings Paul experienced on account of his commitment to Christ.

creation, we are called to work along with God, "with Christ," in resisting and defeating the causes and consequences of sin and suffering.

Despite the extra sufferings required of believers, God's love and not our sufferings may shape our present reality. God's love is seen in Christ's death ("He who did not spare his own Son but gave him up for us all," 8:32). God's love is present in Christ's suffering, and Paul opens our eyes to the reality that God's love is present also in ours, as we suffer "with Christ."

5

CONCLUSION

⸺

At the heart of Paul's gospel is "the word of the cross" (1 Cor 1:18). The cross's presence at the center of his good news means that Paul does not shy away from either the existence or the experience of suffering. He sees clearly that the good news he preaches and lives does *not* promise its converts transformation into super-humans capable of transcending or avoiding the troubles of human existence, *and* that it obligates them to share in God's redeeming project — which is to take on an increase of suffering.

This good news is hard. Its degree of difficulty is seen in the fact that it remains "news" to many contemporary Christian believers — both in what we say about ourselves and how we experience our lives. The prevalence of health and wealth preaching and the confusion and embarrassment that many Christians feel when they encounter difficult times are confirmation that Paul's message is still a hard one to hear. The foreignness to many Christian ears of the tough paradox of the Christian life — that even though suffering is a symptom of sin, those "in Christ" take on an increase of it by virtue of sharing in God's ongoing battle with suffering's source — indicates how effectively we have closed our ears, our hearts, our doors to this hard news.

This hard news is also good. For it offers those who accept it a way of also accepting the difficulties of human existence and of feeling enlivened to struggle toward a place, a time, an experience liberated from distress. The good news Paul announces includes the news that suffering's seemingly intransigent control over existence is, in fact, contingent. Not only will there be an end to suffering, but suffering even now no longer needs to control our lives. Its dominance was diminished through Jesus Christ's death and resurrection. When Christ's suffering — the ultimate suffering of the death of the Son of God — was overcome through his resurrection, suffering's dominance was effectively quashed.

ON THE BASIS of what I have seen in 1 Thessalonians, Philippians, and Romans I would suggest the following about how we may speak about suffering as Christians and about how we might live our lives. What follows is based entirely on the work I have done on three of Paul's letters. There is, of course, much more to say than I do here about Christianity's view of suffering. As many theologians have recognized, Christianity is in some sense all about the problem of suffering. In large measure, the tensions Paul introduces between suffering occasioned by sin and the sufferings that contribute to bringing forth God's new creation have created the dynamics of much Christian thinking. Paul's wrestling with sin as the source of suffering and yet suffering as also productive and even sanctifying has provided the stuff for rich theological work in the years since he wrote. Given that his thoughts have been nuanced and developed over the centuries it can be bracing, even transformative, for us to catch some of them again in their rawness.

Speaking and Living the Heart of the Gospel:
Our Message

Speaking and living our faith in the face of suffering means that we start not with a question — why is this happening? — but with a statement. There is suffering in this world because sin is in this world.

Suffering is not what God wants but what sin wants. The reason Paul is so convinced that sufferings are inherently out of place in God's creation is because he sees sufferings as symptoms of sin. If there were no sin, there would be no sufferings, the ultimate suffering being death. Sin, not God, is the author of the sufferings of human life. If all creation rested in the embrace of God's glory, lived in God's justice, reveled in, breathed, and related through God's life and love (i.e., if all creation were completely freed of sin), there would be no suffering.

Here is no philosophical approach to human sorrows — Paul does not spend energy trying to encourage his hearers to grow into a vision of life that allows sufferings to be seen as inconsequential or even appropriately good, as for instance would Stoicism. Neither does Paul carry into his life "in Christ" some of the answers his Scriptures provided. For example, he does not seek to explain the trials of human afflictions by rooting them in some mysterious plan of the good God,[1] nor does he speak of them here as God's discipline — the purpose of which is to produce repentance.[2]

For Paul suffering is not simply the unfortunate state of things that the wise human should take for granted, accept, and seek to attain a calm response to. Nor is suffering for him a mirage or simply a misinterpretation of the workings of reality based on our tired or skewed vision. Suffering is real. Suffering is indeed suffering — it hurts, it stings, it is an affront to our dignity as human beings, it challenges our sense of our place in the world and our sense of God's care for us. It is not what should be. It is not what we want, nor should want, and it is not what God wants. Suffering is wrong and it is evil — it both offends God's will and is a symptom of the power of sin.

Sin's goal is to separate humanity from God's love by causing the sufferer to question God's character. When a sufferer allows her trust in

1. For instance, some of the Psalms (e.g., Psalm 37 [38]) portray what E. F. Sutcliffe calls a "medicinal" attitude to suffering — the Psalmist sees his suffering as God's reproach for his sins (*Providence and Suffering in the Old and New Testaments* [London: Nelson, 1953], pp. 77 and 86).

2. See, for example, passages in Amos and Jeremiah. For a discussion of this aspect of the Old Testament's view of suffering, see J. A. Sanders, *Suffering as Divine Discipline in the Old Testament and Post-Biblical Judaism* (Rochester: Colgate Rochester Divinity School, 1968).

God to be defeated by the terrifying power of suffering, sin has had its way.

Sin's goal is to kill. Death is the form of suffering that most satisfies sin's ends, for death and the fear of death appear to separate us from life — that force whose source is God. When people die or anticipate death, God's presence or powers may be most doubted. The suffering of *death,* which is the definitive challenge to the presence and possibilities of *life,* epitomizes suffering's capacities to make us feel separate from God.

The sin factor, which manifests itself in suffering, is present both outside our individual beings and within them. Sin is both a power apart from us and a power within each person. This fact makes suffering a given for every part of creation. Paul's gospel dashes all naïveté. We who believe are, then, not surprised at the horrors that occur, and we are not surprised at ourselves when we do things that hurt others or God's good earth.

Paul is concerned about sin not because he is a moralist but because he cares deeply that the world be healed of pain — even of death. Of course, his zeal for this end is rooted in his conviction that this is now assured because God has raised Jesus Christ from the dead.

Our Response

What we are given in Paul's message is, however, not primarily a statement about the source of suffering, but rather a means, a mode for *responding* to the situation of distress in which humanity finds itself.

Suffering Is Wrong and to Be Resisted

Our response may be, if we follow Paul's cue, to feel assured that it is alright to sense that suffering *is* actually out of place in our existence. Suffering is not a part of the human condition that we must learn to accept. It is, rather, foreign to God's plan for creation, and God will ultimately banish it. Our faith that the author of suffering (sin) was mortally wounded by Jesus' death and resurrection and that God's glory will unquestionably obliterate suffering at some good time in the future means that we may legitimate our feelings of dis-ease at our distresses.

Paul's thoughts may encourage us not to feel embarrassed or awkward when we go through the vale of tears that will inevitably shroud our lives at certain points — there is no failure in undergoing suffering. In light of Paul's view that suffering is a symptom of sin, we need not feel ashamed at feeling anger, remorse, grief, fear, or any other such emotion in response to our sorrows. This is a healthy reaction to suffering.

Our faith grants insight. We know the world's pain and we know its cause. We see creation groaning under subjection to life's opposite and we recognize sin as the source of this tragedy. This knowledge is useful to us because it changes our shape from beings who are simply subject to this disaster into people who can resist it. It conforms us, in other words, to Christ.

As God makes manifest, particularly in the revelation of God's righteousness in the gospel, suffering is not to be accepted; it is to be resisted. Through Christ's death and resurrection God demonstrates that the right response to the wrong of suffering is not to succumb to it but to defeat it. Christ's resurrection is the alleviation of Christ's suffering, and the revelation that the divine response/the righteous response to suffering is to proceed through it to life. Consequently, our fitting response to suffering is to resist it.

Resources "in Christ" to Respond to Suffering

Suffering may not oppress us even while it works on us. We are no longer its victims because we need no longer be the victims of sin. "In Christ" we may find resources that allow us not to quake at suffering's sneer because behind the face of pain and death we can see the radiant countenance of God.

We may know ourselves to be "in Christ" and so in God's life. If, as believers, we are convinced that the worst ravages from sin's bite cannot kill the life that is stronger than death, we may undergo the inevitable pain, mental anguish, and experiences of death that are humanity's lot, without granting such suffering sovereignty over us. In fact, we may know peace and joy at the same time as we know suffering, because through us flows God's life — a life that draws us toward life and only life.

Our Hope

We may know that what existence now feels like and looks like is something of a half-truth and is definitely temporary. Now, for both believers in Jesus Christ and others, life in this world includes disease, natural disasters, distress, and death. But this is only partially the truth, for our existence subsequent to Christ's death and resurrection is framed by God's life and love such that even now the troubles of our lives may be experienced in the embrace of the dynamic power of that life and love.

Paul's message is that God in Christ has changed the architecture of existence. Now what supports us when we suffer is both the hope for suffering's end and the reality that sin's (and so suffering's) arrogant dictatorship over humankind has been severely damaged.

"In Christ" we may know the hope of the end of suffering, being convinced that sin, the root of suffering, is not a sustainable resource in God's cosmos. Sin's shelf life was severely limited at the cross and resurrection. And we who are baptized into Christ's death are aware that God's love has proven stronger than sin. Consequently, while now we suffer, along with the rest of humanity, we know that there will come a time when all will be well. And our hope is that this will be the case for all humanity, for all that is.

Our Responsibility

Believers in Christ may live in the presence of the hope of the end of suffering both for ourselves and for those who do not believe. In fact, one of our responsibilities as believers is to believe this for those who cannot. The effect of our believing for the rest of humanity is that we will be able to care for the suffering of others. This changes both us and others. It conforms us to Christ while reshaping existence for others.

Paul's perspective is that those who do not believe in Christ see their suffering only in the context of suffering. We, on the other hand, may see their suffering bounded by God's life and love and by its inevitable abolishment. Because of our insight into suffering's contingency we may / should care for those who feel only dominated by suffering's grip.

The effect of the cross and resurrection is not that suffering is experienced by either Christians or non-Christians any less intensely or horrifically. It remains suffering — that experience that threatens to destroy what is beautiful and peaceful and pleasant in our lives. But those who accept Paul's message no longer suffer in darkness. In Christ, the light of God has broken into the black prison of the world's pain. By sharing our pain in order to defeat the cause of our pain, Christ's cross pierced the darkness. Now even as we suffer we may do so in the knowledge that God's love surrounds us and will eventually liberate us.

While Paul distinguishes between believers and nonbelievers, he does not create a chasm between them. As a believer, Paul not only worries over those who in his view are still mastered by sin and so caught in the jaws of suffering and death, but he also expects believers to identify with those who are not "in Christ." Paul's emphasis that all of humanity shares a common history of trading in sin and so perpetuating suffering, and also a common tribulation at the impending death of our bodies, serves to temper any conceit on the part of the converted that we no longer need to share with, care for, understand, or identify with those who do not believe as we do.

Paul encourages us to feel outrage at and compassion for the suffering of any person or any part of creation, no matter how foreign these people or places are from our current social, geographical, or religious venues. For we are all one, sharing a common experience of the tribulations of sin-infused existence. We are encouraged by Paul not to objectify or diminish the sufferings of those who do not share our faith or who disagree with us, and certainly not to justify inflicting sufferings on those who do not believe as we. Sufferings are wrong; only love changes things for the better.

There is energy available to us as believers — God's energy of love and life, mediated to us by the Holy Spirit. When we ourselves are uncomfortable we may find peace and joy as companions to our sorrows; we may find assurance of God's loving and life-giving presence even when suffering severely challenges all equanimity. This extra energy which comes from bringing our sufferings into Christ, experiencing them "in Christ," frees us not only to undergo our particular trials with hope and a degree of calm, but it also affords us the capacity to reach beyond ourselves and care for others who are hurting.

Paul's message invites us to see ourselves as obligated to suffer along with Christ so that the beam of God's glory, from which sin and suffering must necessarily scurry away, may reach as wide a range as possible. We may then not only bring our sufferings into Christ, but also act along with Christ for God's justice now.

The added difficulties and challenges this will bring to our lives are bearable because we bear them along with Christ and, hopefully, with others who are "in Christ."

Paul's Invitation

Paul's faith allows him to draw a picture of human existence that realistically represents our difficulties while not letting them dominate the scene. Paul's faith means that he chooses a canvas large enough to incorporate not only human troubles but also the vigorous actions of God which are perpetually directed to healing and transforming all that is sick and destructive. The glow of God's life and love, not the pains of our existence, are what primarily catches Paul's eye as he paints his version of reality.

The trust in God that allows Paul to see things the way he does is offered to all. Paul invites us to turn from the inevitable narcissism that attends the troubles we encounter toward the shimmering life of God, which offers us hope and joy and peace even as we suffer. Though we may suffer, suffering may no longer define our existence, for we no longer serve sin, the author and director of suffering. Instead, we serve the God of life, the God of love, the God of righteousness, the one whose raison d'être is to save, whose deepest desire is to heal suffering and death.

We are called to action, to be "with Christ" in engagement on the side of God's justice, and to accept the inevitable sufferings that go along with such engagement. By virtue of suffering "with Christ" we are called to face the darkness, to face down what destroys, to reshape what is so that it comes to be dominated not by suffering but by God's glory. The burden of our vision of the depth of the pain in which creation is caught is to be both borne and used. Where we see suffering and death we are obliged to bring their opposites.

We, of course, do not do this on our own steam. Suffering "with Christ" is to suffer with the Messiah, not to be the Messiah. We are not responsible to be gods to others, but to offer ourselves to be used by God. Our burden to suffer "with Christ," to paraphrase Jesus' words in Matthew, is light. For, we suffer not on our own but *with* the one whose sufferings drew him inexorably into God's luminous life.

Index of Subjects and Names

Assurance in suffering, 67-69, 74
Athletic metaphors/rhetoric: Philippians, 40, 72; Thessalonians, 25-26, 32n.23
Augustine, 50n.36, 67n.76, 94, 94n.53, 111

Baptism, 110
Barth, K.: on future hope, 107n.92; on God's glory/God's love, 101; on Paul's view of death, 90, 91n.46; on Philippians, 51-52n.41, 58, 72n.83; on Romans, 100, 107n.92, 112, 123n.121
Bauer, W., 53n.42
Believers' suffering, 8, 12; acceptance of the gospel/acceptance of suffering, 15-17, 29, 50-52; atypical explanations for, 70-73; being crucified with Christ, 99, 99n.62; and birth of a new age, 18-19, 23-24; and care for others, 24, 73; causes of, 22-24, 31-33, 34; challenge to suffer, 30-31, 33, 34, 35; and Christ-like characteristics, 19-22, 23, 29, 31-33; and Christ's death, 55-59, 99-100, 100n.67; and completion of God's salvific project, 19-22, 29; and death, 118; differences from nonbelievers' suffering, 23,

27-29; embodying Christ's own suffering, 104-5; and eternal life, 123-24; future suffering, 90-91, 114; as gift/ privilege, 61; and God's glory, 101-3, 123, 124-25; and God's love, 101, 102-3, 113-14, 120; and God's righteousness, 102-3, 125-26; and God's wrath, 121; and hope, 19-22, 29, 33, 101-2, 105-8, 116; and humanity's shared suffering, 78-92, 114-15, 117-18; and joy, 17-18, 26-27, 30, 34, 58-59, 62-63, 65; and lack of trust in God, 84-90, 115; and love, 19-22, 29, 32-33, 50, 50n.36, 62-63, 66, 74-75; and martyrdom, 38n.6, 42, 66-67, 66nn.71-72, 67n.75; the mutuality of suffering, 59-61; not sought for its own sake, 26, 29-30, 31, 34; obligation to share in God's care for creation, 126-27; Paul's participation in Christ's suffering, 52-55; Paul's reflections on his own suffering, 38-40; and perfection, 52, 67, 67n.76; Philippians and Paul's suffering, 38-63, 66-75; as productive, 33-34; Romans, 42, 43, 97-114, 115, 116-27; and sanctification, 20, 21, 24-26, 29,

30, 35; and the shape of Christ's afflictions, 18-22, 29; and sin, 79-81, 82, 91, 92, 109-13, 114, 117, 120-21; and suffering in God's life, 99-101; as the suffering of misfits, 32-33; suffering with insight, 108-14, 116; Thessalonians, 15-27, 30-35; as unbidden/not to be provoked, 31; what it's not, 26-27. *See also* "In Christ" suffering; "With Christ" suffering

Bloomquist, L. G., 38n.5, 66n.72

Bockmuehl, M., 38n.5, 59n.60

Bodies: Christ's suffering embodied in believers, 104-5; and future suffering, 91, 91n.48; Paul's bodily afflictions, 54; Philippians, 54; resisting sin's reign in, 110; Romans, 91, 91n.48, 100, 104-5, 110

Bruce, F. F., 31n.22, 55-56n.46

Byrne, B., 93n.52, 109n.100, 123n.121

Calvin, John, 20n68, 33n.24, 46, 82n.23, 91, 107n.95, 124n.126

Cassidy, R., 45n.21, 57n.52

Chronological sequence of Paul's letters, 12n.23

Circumcision, 45n.20, 53, 54

Colombas, G. M., 66n.72

Corinthian correspondence, 11, 47

Cranfield, C. E. B., 82n.25, 85n.31, 85n.33, 91n.47, 100n.69, 103n.80, 112

Cross: and Paul's gospel message, 129; suffering and the cruciform shape of Christian life, 67-68

Death: and human suffering, 80, 91, 99-100, 118; and "in Christ" suffering, 99-100, 100n.67; nonbelievers' grief in face of, 28, 35; Philippians, 55-59, 66; physical, 91, 91n.46; Romans, 80, 91, 99-100, 118, 119; and sin, 80, 91, 91n.47; suffering in conformity with Christ's

death, 55-59, 66; Thessalonians, 28, 35; and the unconverted, 119

De Boer, W. P., 18n.9

Deidun, T. J., 99n.64

Disciples of Jesus, suffering of, 8-9

Donfried, K. P., 22n.16, 31n.22

Dunn, J. D. G., 107n.93, 108n.97

End of suffering: and believer-specific suffering, 18-22, 23-24, 29; and the birth of a new age, 18-19, 23-24; hope in, 134; and horizon of God's reality, 69; nonbelievers and God's wrath, 97; Philippians, 69; Romans, 97; Thessalonians, 18-22, 23-24, 29

"Enemies of the cross of Christ," 46-47, 47n.25, 64

Epaphroditus, 60

Faith: as armor against darkness, 21-22; the choice to exercise, 32-33; Christ-like characteristic of, 19-22, 23, 28, 29, 31-33; and the coming kingdom, 21; energies of, 32-33; increasing exhibition of, 20-21; and nonbelievers' suffering, 28; productive conflicts arising from, 33-34

Fee, G. D., 40n.10, 55n.46, 59n.61, 63n.68, 67n.73

Fitzmyer, J., 91n.48, 103n.79, 110n.101, 124n.127

Fowl, S., 37n.2, 42n.17

Frame, J. E., 19n.11

Future suffering: of nonbelievers, 63-64, 90-91, 114; Philippians, 63-64; Romans, 90-91, 105-8, 114, 116; and suffering "with Christ," 105-8, 116

Galatians, Paul's letter to, 53

Garland, D. E., 44n.18

Garlington, D. B., 84n.27

Girard, R., 7n.12

Gnilka, J., 46n.24

Grieb, A. K., 87n.39

Grundmann, W., 79

Hamerton-Kelly, R., 7n.12

Hawthorne, G. F., 46n.24, 60n.62

Haymo of Halberstadt, Bishop, 67n.74

Hays, R. B., 86n.34, 88n.40

Headlam, A., 124n.122

"Hermeneutics of suspicion," 4, 4n.8

"Hermeneutics of sympathy," 4, 4n.8

Hope: as armor against darkness, 21-22; the choice to persevere in, 33; Christ-like characteristic of, 19-22, 23, 28, 29, 31-33; and the coming kingdom, 21; and the end of suffering, 134; energy of, 32-33; future, 105-8, 116; and "in Christ" suffering, 101-2; increasing exhibition of, 20-21; and nonbelievers' suffering, 28, 118-19; present, 106-8, 116; productive conflicts arising from, 33-34; Romans and believers' suffering, 101-2, 105-8, 116; Thessalonians, 19-22, 23, 28, 29, 31-33; "with Christ" suffering, 105-8, 116

Hurtado, L., 57n.51

Ignatius of Antioch, 58n.56, 66n.71

"In Christ" suffering: being united with Christ's death, 99-100, 100n.67; facing our own physical death, 100; and God's glory, 101-3; and God's love, 101-3, 115, 120; and God's righteousness, 102-3, 102n.78, 121n.119; and God's wrath, 121, 121n.119; and love, 50, 50n.36; and nonbelievers' suffering, 134-36; Paul's suffering in Philippians, 43-44, 48-50, 68, 73-74; positive effects, 49-50; producing hope, 101-2; and resources to respond to suffering, 133-34; and Romans, 42, 92, 98-103, 115, 120-22; and sin, 92, 99, 120-21; as suffering in

God's life, 99-101; transformed into something creative and promising, 100

Irenaeus, 67n.76

Jewett, R., 46n.22, 80, 104n.81

Jews: as creating suffering, 96; disobedience/lack of trust in God, 84-85, 84n.28, 87-88; faith/the law and relationship to God, 95, 95nn.55-56; as representative of all nonbelievers, 87-88; and sin, 83, 94-96; as subject to God's wrath, 97; suffering of (as nonbelievers), 94-97

Joy: the communion of suffering and, 58-59, 62-63, 65; paradox of joyful response to suffering, 66, 74-75; and Paul's suffering/imprisonment, 58-59, 65; Philippians, 58-59, 62-63, 65, 66, 74-75; Thessalonians and believer-specific suffering, 17-18, 26-27, 30, 34; Thessalonians and nonbelievers' suffering, 28

Käsemann, E., 78n.4, 82n.23, 83, 85n.30, 105, 107n.92, 109n.99, 110, 126

Keck, L., 81, 86

Klijn, A. J. F., 46n.24

Lewis, C. S., 10

Lightfoot, J. B., 40n.11, 67n.76

Lohmeyer, E., 38n.6, 42

Love: as armor against darkness, 21-22; the choice to labor in, 32-33; Christ-like characteristic of, 19-22, 23, 28, 29, 31-33; and the coming kingdom, 21; energy of, 32-33; God's, 101-3, 113-14, 115, 120; increasing exhibition of, 20-21; and nonbelievers' suffering, 28, 29, 30, 36, 119, 136; Philippians and believers' suffering, 50, 50n.36, 62-63, 66, 74-75; productive conflicts arising from, 33-34; Romans, 101-3, 113-14, 115, 120; and suffering "in Christ," 101-3, 115, 120; and suffering "with Christ," 113-14; Thessalonians, 19-22, 23, 28, 29, 30, 31-33, 36

Luke, Gospel of, 8-9

Luther, Martin, 86, 89n.43, 93n.50, 100n.67, 111

Manson, T. W., 60n.62

Mark, Gospel of, 8n.14

Martin, R. P., 39n.9

Martydom, 38n.6, 42, 66-67, 66nn.71-72, 67n.75

Martyn, J. L., 79n.6, 81n.22

Matthew, Gospel of, 8-9, 8n.14

McGill, Arthur C., 10

Meeks, W. A., 61n.66

Minear, P. S., 38n.6, 39n.7

Müller-Bardoff, J., 46n.24

Mutuality of suffering, 59-61, 66

"New perspective" scholarship, 95n.55

Nonbelievers' suffering, 8, 12, 27-29, 30; creating suffering, 96; distinctive kinds of, 8, 28-29, 30; distinctive manner of, 27-28; "enemies of the cross of Christ," 46-47, 47n.25, 64; future human suffering, 63-64, 90-91, 114; and God's wrath, 8n.13, 28-29, 28n.21, 30, 97; grief in the face of death, 28, 35; and humanity's shared suffering, 78-92, 114-15, 117-18, 135; Jews, 94-97; and lack of trust in God, 84-85, 87-88; and love, 28, 29, 30, 36, 119, 136; Philippians on, 63-64, 65; and practice of evil, 83; present human suffering, 82-83; responding to, 29, 30, 35-36, 119, 134-36; and Romans, 78n.2, 82-97, 115, 117-19; and sin, 79-81, 82, 83, 92-94, 114-15, 115, 118-19; and spread of suffering, 92-94; Thessalonians, 27-29, 30, 35-36; those who acknowledge God but not Christ,

94-96; those who do not acknowledge God at all, 94; and ungodliness, 82-83, 82n.25; without hope, 28, 118-19; without joy, 28

O'Brien, P. T., 56n.47

Perfection and suffering, 52, 67, 67n.76

Perkins, P., 42n.17

Persecutions in Thessalonica, 31n.22

Pfitzner, V. C., 17n.6

Philippians and nonbelievers' suffering, 63-64, 65; "enemies of the cross of Christ," 46-47, 47n.25, 64; future suffering, 63-64

Philippians and Paul's suffering as a believer, 11-12, 37-75; accepting suffering and gaining Christ, 50-52; ambiguity and interpretive challenges, 42-44; assurance in suffering, 67-69, 74; athletic images/metaphors, 40, 72; atypical explanations, 70-73; and bodily afflictions, 54; and Christ's God-bestowed name, 57n.51; and Christ's suffering, 52-57, 73-74; and circumcision, 45n.20, 53, 54; and conformity with Christ's death, 55-59; and the cross, 67-68; and the end of suffering, 69; and "enemies," 46-47, 47n.25, 64; exhortation to the Philippians, 61; and form of Christ's death, 55-59, 57n.52; gift/privilege of suffering, 61; and glorifying God, 57; and joy, 58-59, 62-63, 65, 66, 74-75; and letter to the Romans, 42, 43; and letter to the Thessalonians, 39; loss of one's past and new life "in" Christ, 51, 51nn.40-41, 65; love and understanding suffering, 50, 50n.36, 62-63, 66, 74-75; martyrdom, 38n.6, 42, 66-67, 66nn.71-72, 67n.75; mutuality of suffering, 59-61, 66; Paul's apology/defense, 42-61, 64; Paul's imprisonment, 37-38,

40-41, 65; Paul's jailers, 41n.14, 48n.33, 49; Paul's mental anguish, 41; Paul's self-defensive tone, 45-48; and perfection, 52, 67, 67n.76; Philippians' participation in Paul's suffering, 60, 60n.63; the Philippians' suffering, 59-60; positive effects of Christ's suffering/death, 55-57, 56n.49, 66; and salvation of others, 73; scholarly questions of the letter's integrity, 38n.5; scorning avoidance of suffering, 47-48; and Stoicism, 37-38, 62, 69, 72; suffering and sanctification, 52; suffering as neither punishment nor purge, 70-72; suffering "in Christ," 43-44, 48-50, 68, 73-74; suffering with Christ," 43-44; and victimization/persecution, 48-49, 65, 69; ways Philippians should *not* be used, 69

Polycarp, 67n.77

Predestination, 88n.41

Problematic theology, 10-11

Q document, 8n.14

Responding to suffering, 2, 132-36; finding resources "in Christ," 133-34; hope in the end of suffering, 134; realizing that suffering is wrong/to be resisted, 132-33; the suffering of nonbelievers, 29, 30, 35-36, 119, 134-36; using God's energy of love, 136

Ricoeur, P., 3n.3

Righteousness of God: "in Christ" context and sharing in, 93-94, 93n.50; Romans, 84-90, 93-94, 102-3, 102n.78, 115, 125-26; the suffering of lack of trust in, 84-90, 115; and suffering "with Christ," 125-26

Romans and human suffering, 11-13, 77-127; Christ's suffering embodied in believers, 104-5; and death, 80, 91, 91n.46, 99-100, 118; disobedience/obedience of faith, 84-85, 84nn.27-28, 87-88; and the future, 90-91, 105-8, 114, 116; and God's glory, 101-3, 115, 123, 124-25; and God's love, 101-3, 113-14, 115, 120; and God's righteousness, 102-3, 102n.78; and God's wrath, 82, 97, 121, 121n.119; history of suffering, 90, 114; and hope, 106-8, 116; and human dignity, 117; humanity's shared suffering, 78-92, 114-15, 117-18; and lack of trust in God, 84-90, 115; and practice of evil, 83; and predestination, 88n.41; present suffering, 82-83; and righteousness of God, 84-90, 93-94, 102-3, 102n.78, 115, 125-26; sin and nonbelievers, 82, 83, 92, 94-96, 118-19; sin and suffering, 79-81, 90, 109-13, 114, 116, 117, 120-21; suffering "in Christ," 42, 92, 98-103, 115, 120-22; suffering in God's life, 99-101; suffering of believers, 42, 43, 97-114, 115; suffering of nonbelievers, 78n.2, 82-97, 115, 117-19; suffering "with Christ," 42, 99n.62, 103-14, 115-16, 122-27; suffering with insight, 108-14, 116; and ungodliness, 82-83, 82n.25

Sanctification and suffering: Philippians, 52; Thessalonians, 20, 21, 24-26, 29, 30, 35

Sanday, W., 124n.122

Sanders, E. P., 95n.55, 99n.62

Schweitzer, A., 5n.10, 98n.61

Scott, J. M., 124n.124

Silva, M., 57n.51

Sin, 130-32; the believer's struggle against, 111-13; and death, 80, 91, 91n.47; and decay, 80-81, 80n.13; distinct relationships to, 82, 83, 92, 111-13; and humanity's shared suffering, 79-81; and Manichean agenda, 81; and nonbelievers, 82, 83, 92-96, 118-19; and the obedience of faith, 113; as power beyond human control, 81; resisting reign in our bodies, 110; as root of human suffering, 79-80, 114; and suffering "in Christ," 92, 99, 120-21; and suffering "with Christ," 109-13, 116

Spirit of God, 107

Stendahl, K., 3

Stoicism, 37-38, 62, 69, 72, 131

Stowers, S., 44-45n.19, 85n.32

Stuhlmacher, P., 110, 110n.102

"Suffering" (defining), 3-4, 4nn.5-7

Suffering, studying Paul's understanding of, 1-13; amateur theological reflections, 9-10; the approach of this book, 3-5; appropriating Paul's response, 2; categorizing Pauline passages, 8; and communication with nonbelievers, 7; exegetical analyses, 2-3; "hermeneutics of sympathy," 4, 4n.8; interpreting what the texts might mean, 9-10, 9n.16; interpretive care and avoiding misreading, 5-7; the organization and scope of this book, 8-13; and Paul's relevance, 4-5; preventative reasons, 5-7; and "problematic theology," 10-11; productive reasons, 5-7; thematic approach, 5; the three letters chosen for study, 11-13; tools of critical biblical scholarship, 3; why this investigation matters, 5-8

Sutcliffe, E. F., 131n.1

Tertullian, 67n.75

Thessalonians, 11-12, 15-36; first thanksgiving section, 15n.2, 16-17, 39; and the letter to the Philippians, 39; Paul's athletic rhetoric, 25-26, 32n.23; and victimhood/victimization, 32n.23

Thessalonians and believer-specific suffering, 15-27, 30-35; acceptance of gospel as acceptance of suffering, 15-17, 29; and birth of a new age, 18-19, 23-24; the causes of suffering, 22-24, 31-33, 34; the challenge to suffer, 30-31, 33, 34, 35; characteristics of faith, hope, and love, 19-22, 23, 29, 31-33; and completion of God's salvific project, 19-22, 29; and the end of all suffering, 23-24; and imitation of Christ, 15, 18, 18n.9, 24; and joy, 17-18, 26-27, 30, 34; living quietly/avoiding provocative behavior, 22-23, 29-30; productive suffering, 33-34; references to the faith of Jesus, 17-18, 17n.8; the shape of afflictions, 18-22, 29; suffering and sanctification, 20, 21, 24-26, 29, 30, 35; suffering not sought for its own sake, 26, 29-30, 31, 34; what believer-specific suffering is not, 26-27, 29-30, 34

Thessalonians and nonbelievers' suffering, 27-29, 30, 35-36; differences from suffering of believers, 23, 27-29; distinctive kinds of suffering, 28-29, 30; distinctive manner of suffering, 27-28; experiencing God's coming wrath, 28-29, 28n.21, 30; facing suffering without hope, faith, or love, 28; facing suffering without joy, 28; grieving in the face of death, 28, 35; making Paul's response our own, 36; Paul's care/compassion, 29, 30, 35-36; the suffering specific to nonbelievers, 27-29, 30

Trust: believers' lack of, 85-86; nonbelievers' lack of, 84-85, 87-88; Paul's invitation to, 136-37; Romans, 84-90, 115; the suffering of lack of trust in God's righteousness, 84-90, 115

Ungodliness, 82-83, 82n.25

Victimhood and victimization: Philippians, 48-49, 65, 69; Thessalonians, 32n.23

Violence in human society, 7n.12

Wedderburn, A. J. M., 105n.84

Westerholm, S., 95n.56

"With Christ" suffering: bearing the wait with patience, 124, 124n.126; being crucified with Christ, 99n.62; embodiment of Christ's suffering, 104-5; and eternal life, 123-24; and God's glory, 123, 124-25; and hope (future), 105-6, 116; and hope (present), 106-8, 116; with insight, 108-14, 116; meaning for God/God's creation, 124-27; meaning for us, 122-24; Paul's invitation to, 137; Philippians and Paul's suffering, 43-44;

Romans, 42, 99n.62, 103-14, 115-16, 122-27; serving God's righteousness/justice, 125-26; serving the glory of God, 124-25, 124n.128; and sin, 109-13, 116

Wrath of God: and God's righteousness, 121n.119; and humanity's shared suffering, 82; and nonbelievers' suffering, 8n.13, 28-29, 28n.21, 30, 97; Romans, 82, 97, 121, 121n.119; and suffering "in Christ," 121; Thessalonians, 28-29, 28n.21, 30

Wright, N. T., 58n.53

Index of Scripture References

OLD TESTAMENT/
HEBREW BIBLE

Genesis
3:17   81

Psalms
37 [38]   131n.1

Isaiah
45:23   57n.52

APOCRYPHA

4 Ezra
4:42   19

1 Enoch
62:4   19

NEW TESTAMENT

Matthew
10:34-39   5

John
16:21   19

Romans
1:5   84nn.27-28
1:16   93, 95
1:16-17   103, 126
1:16-18   112
1:17   89, 102n.78
1:18   82, 121n.119
1:18-31   94
1:21   118
1:22   82
1:24   79n.10, 82, 83,
                    84n.28, 94, 101
1:24-32   79n.5, 90
1:26   83
1:28   83
1:29   83
1:29-31   83

1:32   80
2:5   97, 119, 121n.119
2:6-7   82n.23
2:7   94
2:8   97
2:9   97
2:17-24   83
2:21-23   95
3:5-6   97
3:5-7   94
3:9   79, 93, 94
3:10   79
3:16   96
3:19   94
3:20   95
3:21   102n.78, 110
3:21-22   93
3:21-26   117
3:22   17, 93n.51
3:23   106n.88
3:23-25a   124
3:23-25   56n.40
3:26   102
4:7   79n.5
4:24-25   94

146

4:25	94n.53	7:9-24	114	8:35	80n.14, 109, 110,
5:1	87, 99, 103	7:10	112, 113		113, 114, 126
5:1-11	87n.36	7:12-13	112	8:35b	109n.100
5:2	103, 106	7:14	82, 107n.95, 112	8:37	113, 114
5:3	102	7:19	83	8:38-39a	109n.100
5:3-4	101	7:23	112	8:39	101, 106, 113
5:5	101, 126	7:24–8:1	123	9–11	84, 85-86
5:8-9	102	7:24	91n.48	9:1-3	89, 108
5:8-10	114n.114	8:1	96	9:2	95
5:9	97, 103, 121	8:2	119	9:5	84
5:9-10	108	8:3	107n.95	9:6–11:10	97
5:10	101, 103	8:9	99, 107	9:11	89
5:12	80	8:10	91, 108	9:12-14	89
5:12-14	99	8:11	91, 100	9:13	89
5:13	111	8:12	93	9:14	89, 121
5:17	91	8:14-17	104n.81	9:15	88, 89
5:17-21	100	8:15	118n.116	9:19	85n.32
5:20	79n.5, 111	8:16	103	9:32	95
6:1-11	100, 112	8:16-17	106	10:1	84, 85, 87
6:2	103	8:17	78n.4, 99n.62, 103nn.79-80, 104, 108, 110n.101, 122, 123	10:1-4	86
6:3	92, 121			10:3	84, 89
6:3-11	99n.62			10:12	87
6:4	92, 100			10:21	84
6:5	99	8:17-18	104	11:5	88n.41
6:6	99	8:18	78, 101	11:7	88n.41
6:7	99n.65, 109	8:19-23	105	11:11-12	84
6:10	99	8:20	81	11:13	85
6:11	99, 100, 109	8:21	80, 108, 125	11:19	85
6:12	110	8:22	19, 78n.3, 108	11:25	85, 86, 121
6:13	100, 110	8:23	78n.3, 104n.85, 107, 108n.6	11:26	96
6:18	79n.9, 111, 112, 126			11:27	79n.5
6:22	112	8:25	124	11:28-31	88
6:22-23	110	8:26	107	11:29	88
7	83	8:27	107	11:31	84
7:5	79n.5, 119	8:28	121n.120	11:32	84n.28, 87, 89n.43
7:7-25	111, 113	8:28-29	109	11:33	90
7:8	112n.111	8:29	104, 106	11:33-36	121
7:8b	111	8:30	123	12:1	110
7:9a	111	8:31-39	120	12:9-13	101
7:9b	112	8:32	102, 106, 110, 113, 125, 127	12:21	126
7:9-13	112n.111			13:12	110, 121n.119
				13:14	110

15:3	124	1:25	58n.58, 60	3:8	50, 67n.73
15:7	124	1:27	40n.13	3:8b	50n.37
15:7-12	85n.31	1:27-28	48n.33, 61, 64	3:8-9	68
15:8	95	1:28	49, 63	3:8b-9	50
15:13	107	1:28-30	59	3:9	17, 51, 65, 70
15:17	124	1:29	57	3:10	19, 43, 53, 54, 55,
		1:29-30	52, 61		56n.47, 57, 65,
1 Corinthians		1:30	40n.13, 62, 69		103n.79
1:9	68	2:1	53n.45	3:10-11	54, 56
1:18	129	2:2	58n.57	3:11	43, 54, 66
4:8	47	2:5-8	61	3:12	50n.37, 51, 52, 62
13:13	21	2:5-11	39	3:12-14	39, 40n.13
15:12	47	2:6-8	39	3:13-14	25
15:24-28	63	2:6-11	47	3:14	52
		2:8	40, 47, 59, 67n.76	3:18	46, 47, 64
Galatians		2:9-10	57n.51	3:18-19	47n.25
2:16	17	2:9-11	56	3:19	47, 63
2:20	57	2:10-11	57	3:21	40
		2:11	56, 57, 63	4:1	58n.57
Philippians		2:12	40n.13	4:3	40n.13
1:3-11	45	2:12-13	51	4:4	58n.58
1:4	58n.57	2:16	40n.13, 67n.77	4:10	58n.57
1:7	40	2:17	58nn.57-58, 59,	4:11	39
1:7b	56		60, 66n.17	4:11-13	62
1:9	50, 62	2:17-18	62	4:12	40
1:12	45, 49n.35	2:18	58n.58	4:13	41n.15
1:13	40, 43, 48, 52, 60,	2:19-25	37n.1	4:14	60
	65	2:23-24	58	4:15-17	60
1:13-14	49	2:26	60	4:18	60
1:14	40, 41, 50	2:27	60		
1:15	41n.14, 45	2:28	58n.58	**Colossians**	
1:15-17	41	2:29	58n.58	1:18-20	104n.83
1:16	44n.18, 46, 50,	2:30	60	1:24	104, 105n.84
	56n.50, 62	3:1	58n.58		
1:17	40, 41, 45	3:2	46	**1 Thessalonians**	
1:18	41, 58n.57	3:2-6	47n.25	1:2-5	15n.2
1:19	58, 60, 67n.76	3:2-10	45n.20	1:2-10	15, 16
1:20	40, 54, 57, 67n.74	3:3	53	1:3	19, 20, 21, 23, 28
1:21	59	3:4-6	53	1:4	18, 23
1:22	59n.59	3:4-11	51n.41	1:5	17, 24
1:23	58n.56, 59	3:7	50	1:6	15, 16, 17, 19, 20,
1:24	59	3:7-10	39		21, 24, 26, 27

Index of Scripture References

1:7	26	3:3-4	17, 26	4:16	21, 31n.22
1:9	15	3:4	16	4:17	21
1:9-10	19	3:4-6	21	5:2	35
1:10	19, 20, 33	3:5	20	5:3	19, 32
2:2	17, 25	3:6	16, 21, 26	5:5	22
2:4	25	3:12	20n.14, 29, 36	5:6	28
2:9-10	25	3:12-13	20, 21	5:6-7	28
2:12	20, 21, 23	4:9	24	5:8	21, 22, 32
2:13-16	16	4:9-10	26	5:8-9	20, 23
2:14	17, 21, 26, 31, 35	4:10	20n.14	5:9	19
2:14-16	18, 29	4:12	20n.14, 22	5:10	19, 34
2:16b	28n.21	4:13	28, 35	5:18	20n.14
3:3	21	4:14-17	19	5:23	27